RAGING BULLS!

NBA CHAMPS

Michael Bradley

Tim Povtak

Nick Rousso

Saul Wisnia

PUBLICATIONS INTERNATIONAL, LTD.

Louis Weber, C.E.O.
Publications International, Ltd.
7373 North Cicero Avenue
Lincolnwood, Illinois 60646

Manufactured in U.S.A.

8 7 6 5 4 3 2 1

ISBN: 0-7853-2022-9

The Bulls celebrate their NBA-record 70th win after defeating the Milwaukee Bucks April 16.

Michael Bradley is a freelance writer and radio analyst whose written work has appeared in *The Sporting News, Sport, College Sports, Slam,* and *The Philadelphia Inquirer.* He is also a contributor to the One-On-One Radio Network.

Tim Povtak is a sports columnist and NBA writer for *The Orlando Sentinel.* He has covered the NBA since 1989. He is co-author of *Meet Shaquille O'Neal* and a contributing writer to *The Sporting News, Street & Smith's,* and *Beckett* trading card magazine.

Nick Rousso is editor of *Ultimate Sports Basketball.* He is the former editor of *Dick Vitale's Basketball* and *Don Heinrich's College Football* and was an associate editor for *Bill Mazeroski's Baseball, The Show,* and *Don Heinrich's Pro Preview.*

Saul Wisnia is a former sports and feature writer for *The Washington Post.* He has written for *Sports Illustrated, The Boston Globe, Boston Herald,* and *Boston Red Sox Scorebook Magazine* and was editor of the Boston Bruins' fan magazine.

CONTENTS

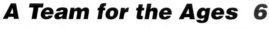

A TEAM FOR THE AGES

Years from now, we'll tell our grandkids about the greatest team we ever saw— the 1995-96 Chicago Bulls.

This is the team that we'll re-member. This is The One. Years from now, on a rainy Sunday afternoon, when the grandkids are bored and ripe for a story, we'll gather 'em around the table and say, "Kids, let me tell you a tale about the most amazing team there ever was—the 1995-96 Chicago Bulls."

Thinking back to the Bulls, mem-ories will gush through our minds. We'll begin to spout buzzwords popular at the time: "70" and "72," "Oprah" and "Madonna," "Wilt's Lakers" and the "Dancing Rod-mans." The kids will look at us as if

we were nuts, but then we'll settle down and tell them the whole story.

We'll start with Michael Jordan, a basketball god so larger than life that—when he made his second coming during the 1995 Lenten sea-son—a Roman Catholic priest re-ferred to the event as "Michael Jordan Weekend." We'll remember the night early in the 1995-96 sea-son when Jordan torched the expan-sion Vancouver Grizzlies for 19 points in the final six minutes, leav-ing Western Canadians wondering what they had gotten themselves into. We'll recall the day in January

when Philadelphia rookie Jerry Stackhouse proclaimed that no one could guard him, "not even Michael Jordan," and how MJ went and outscored the cocky rookie 48-13. We'll remember the early rounds of the playoffs when Jordan, his back racked with pain, posted games of 44 and 46 points while spending his respites laid out on the floor.

The Bulls, we'll tell the kids, were as awesome as the player who led them, starting 5-0, 10-1, and 23-2 on their way to surpassing the 1971-72 Lakers (69-13) for the greatest record in NBA history. Bulls Mania swept the nation. From Seattle to Miami, fans begged to touch the garments of Jordan and his fellow Bulls super-stars, Scottie Pippen and Dennis Rodman. So great was the hysteria that broadcaster Danny Ainge re-ferred to the team as "the Beatles."

If Michael Jordan was the Paul McCartney of this Magical Mystery Tour, then Scottie Pippen was John Lennon. Pippen rocked the New

Left: On April 16, throngs of Chicagoans drove up to Milwaukee to celebrate history in the making. The Bulls beat the Bucks 86-80 for their record 70th victory. Right: Flight No. 23 took off frequently in 1995-96, leaving foes awestruck.

With his long strides and lightning quickness, Scottie Pippen exploded to the hole faster than foes could react.

House on Madison all year long, rattling rims as well as his opponents with his spectacular dunks. While most thought Jordan was the league's Most Valuable Player, others cast their votes for Pippen. We'll never forget that February afternoon in Indianapolis when Pip and MJ combined for 84 points, ruining Sunday dinners all across Indiana.

The personalities of the Bulls ran the gamut. There was coach Phil Jackson, in his scholarly beard and glasses, who looked like he'd be more at home at a metaphysics seminar than coaching the Triangle

Offense; Toni Kukoc, a 6'10" Croatian known as the "Pink Panther" for his long legs and catlike agility; Luc Longley, a 7'2" giant with a dainty Australian accent; and Steve Kerr, looking more like your paperboy than the greatest triple bomber in NBA history. Suiting up, too, were Canadian Bill Wennington, Ron "Hollywood" Harper, and three former Detroit Piston Bad Boys— John "Spider" Salley, James "Buddha" Edwards, and, of course, Dennis "The Menace" Rodman.

Ah, Dennis Rodman. . . . We'll remember Dennis like we would an

explosion at the Pittsburgh Paint Company. The hair came in many colors: green, pink, blond, orange, red, and orange and red swirl. Tattoos decorated his muscular frame, while earrings pierced his flesh from nose to navel.

But oh, how people loved him! Madonna, he claimed, wanted to have his child. His fans arrived at games with pink hair, tattooed shirts, and, in one case, a Dennis-O-Meter to keep track of Rodman's many rebounds. When Dennis began a ritual of giving away his jersey after games, fans clamored around him, screaming and waving homemade signs that begged for his clothing: "Hey Dennis! I'll Pierce My Bellybutton For Your Jersey." When Rodman gave his shirt to Oprah Winfrey after a game, Oprah jumped up and down, giddy as a schoolgirl.

As the Bulls' win total climbed skyward—41-3, 54-6—the United Center became the hottest ticket in show business. As in previous years, player introductions were as spectacular as a Michael Jackson concert, with throbbing music, shooting lights, and the hyped voice of the P.A. announcer blaring through the din of the crowd, "AT GUARD, SIX-FOOT-SIX OUT OF NORTH CAROLINA. . . ."

With the Bulls winning their first 37 home games of the season, fans' interest wandered to sideshows: M&M races on the big screen; the Bulls' mascot doing the trampoline slam; injured forward Jack Haley,

Fifty years from now, these kids will still be talking about Kerr's 3s and Jordan's jams.

acquired from San Antonio to be Rodman's babysitter, waving his white towel from the Chicago bench. During one game, former Bulls star Bob Love got married at halftime.

When the Bulls won their NBA-record 70th game on April 16 at Milwaukee, we began to see things we had never seen before. As the Bulls' bus motored north to the cheese state, fans hung over expressway overpasses cheering them

on while a TV news chopper hovered above. Jay Leno and his *Tonight Show* blew into the Windy City and kicked off the week with the Dancing Rodmans, who bopped about the stage in No. 91 jerseys and multicolored, glow-in-the-dark hair. And when Dennis had a book-signing for *Bad as I Wanna Be,* he arrived on his motorcycle, his face painted like a drag queen's and a pink boa draped around his shoulders as if he were Ginger on *Gilligan's Island.*

But perhaps what we'll remember most is simply the image of the Bulls bringing the ball up the court: Michael dribbling at the top of the arc, guarded by some scared kid who hoped he wouldn't get embarrassed too badly. Pippen on the wing, ready to explode to the hoop for an alley-oop slam. Little Steve Kerr scurrying around for an open 3-point shot. And Rodman posturing for a rebound and tip-in of any shot that might miss.

We'll remember the expressions on the faces of the opponents— humble, serious, concerned. They knew they were in for it those nights. They knew they were facing the greatest club they had ever played. These were the 1995-96 Chicago Bulls, we'll tell the kids, the best team there ever was.

Though he disturbed some adults with his multihued hair and his numerous tattoos, Dennis Rodman hit it off great with the kids.

SOARIN' TO 72

Jordan gets back in shape, Rodman keeps his head on straight, and the Bulls romp to a record 72 victories.

In the beginning, before a single ball was bounced in earnest, 70 wins wasn't even a consideration. There was too much else to worry about besides chasing immortality. There were questions about whether Dennis Rodman, whose personality covered a spectrum broader than that available to his hairdresser, would detonate at midseason and ruin the Bulls' chemistry. There was concern about the center spot. About the point-guard position. There were even—gasp!—those who wondered whether Michael Jordan's dazzling days were through.

Members of the 1971-72 Los Angeles Lakers, who had set an NBA record with 69 wins in a season, weren't being contacted for interviews about whether their record was in jeopardy. Wilt Chamberlain probably would have scoffed at the prospect of a team without a dominant pivotman assaulting such a lofty achievement.

The Bulls would be good, that was certain. They would probably

Left: *NBC's Marv Albert raved about the Bulls' intensity: "I've never seen a team [get so] sky-high for every game."* **Right:** *Scottie Pippen and the Bulls won at Orlando on Easter Sunday to improve to 66-8.*

be great. But that greatness would not be defined until the playoffs, when Jordan, Rodman, and Scottie Pippen would finally have blended their vast talents into a concoction too lethal for consumption by any other NBA team. The regular season would be but a mere laboratory for the development of a creature capable of wreaking havoc in the post-season.

"On paper, this could be our best team ever," Jordan said early in the season. "The challenge for us right now is to jell as a team. We have so many new people aboard, and it's going to take time for us to become a real team that plays well together every night."

Time would be necessary, because too much had to be discerned before outlandish concepts like 70 wins could be entertained. Reality told us that Jordan had stumbled when he returned to the game in March 1995 after more than a year and a half of humility in baseball's bush leagues. The critics were justified in their questions about whether Jordan was no longer superhuman at age 32. "I second-guessed myself after that, which is something new for me," Jordan allowed after the 1994-95 season had completed.

Jordan's 17-month hiatus from basketball had created a void into which the Houston Rockets had stepped, winning two championships. Their second title came at the expense of the Orlando Magic, who seemed close to taking their place atop the NBA totem pole. The Bulls weren't dead, but they were in need of a full-force, completely rested Jordan. They didn't have that in 1994-95, and they suffered.

"Mentally I knew what I wanted to do last year, but physically I couldn't do it," Jordan told *Basket-*

Despite lacking a true point guard and a legitimate starting center, Phil Jackson's offense ran like clockwork. It's no wonder he was named NBA Coach of the Year.

ball America. "I took for granted a lot of things last year. Coming from baseball and swinging at curveballs and sliders and then, within a month or so, I was shooting basketballs. My body hadn't had the opportunity to adjust, and mentally and physically I wasn't on the same level. I saw the hole, but I couldn't get to it, because it took so much time mentally to send a signal to the physical aspect."

So, there was that. There was also the question of how Pippen would handle a re-relegation to second banana. With Jordan back and clearly playing the lead, Pippen would once again have to sublimate himself to Jordan for the good of the team. It wouldn't be easy. That's why you don't see Robert De Niro taking too many supporting roles.

And then there was Rodman, who arrived in Chicago with more baggage than a brigade of supermodels. He came with a rap sheet of on- and off-court mayhem that had led to his banishment from first Detroit and then San Antonio. Introducing him into the sublime Jordan-Pippen rubric was like hiring Ozzy Osbourne to entertain at the Junior League Ball.

"This was not a snap judgment," Chicago coach Phil Jackson told

The most anticipated game of the year occurred February 2, as Michael Jordan (left) and Magic Johnson (right) met for the first time since 1991. Neither player starred, though, and the Bulls won a ho-hummer, 99-84.

Sports Illustrated before the season. "There are rules and regulations, and we'll ask him to conform." Easier said than done, Coach. Something was going to happen; you just didn't know what or when. Of course, Rodman was on his best behavior when he joined the team and even charmed Chicagoans with his witty sound bites.

"They've already got (Toni) Kukoc, Pippen, and Jordan," Rodman told *SI*. "That's a winning team as it is. Bring somebody like me in, you know, and it just adds a little more cinnamon to the French toast."

The rest of the Bulls were just complements, even former European superstar Kukoc, who was now relegated to sing backup for

BULLS' 1995-96 TEAM STATISTICS

Player	G	MIN	FGs FG	FGs PCT	FTs FT	FTs PCT	3-PT FGs FG	3-PT FGs PCT	Rebounds OFF	Rebounds TOT	AST	STL	TO	BLK	PF	PTS	PPG
Jordan	82	3090	916	.495	548	.834	111	.427	148	543	352	180	197	42	195	2491	30.4
Pippen	77	2825	563	.463	220	.679	150	.374	152	496	452	133	207	57	198	1496	19.4
Kukoc	81	2103	386	.490	206	.772	87	.403	115	323	287	64	114	28	150	1065	13.1
Longley	62	1641	242	.482	80	.777	0	.000	104	318	119	22	114	84	223	564	9.1
Kerr	82	1919	244	.506	78	.929	122	.515	25	110	192	63	42	2	109	688	8.4
Harper	80	1886	234	.467	98	.705	28	.269	74	213	208	105	73	32	137	594	7.4
Rodman	64	2088	146	.480	56	.528	3	.111	356	952	160	36	138	27	196	351	5.5
Wennington	71	1065	169	.493	37	.860	1	1.00	58	174	46	21	37	16	171	376	5.3
Haley	1	7	2	.333	1	.500	0	.000	1	2	0	0	1	0	2	5	5.0
Salley	42	673	63	.450	59	.694	0	.000	46	140	54	19	55	27	110	185	4.4
Buechler	74	740	112	.463	14	.636	40	.444	45	111	56	34	39	7	70	278	3.8
Simpkins	60	685	77	.481	61	.629	1	1.00	66	156	38	9	56	8	78	216	3.6
Edwards	28	274	41	.373	16	.615	0	.000	15	40	11	1	21	8	61	98	3.5
Caffey	57	545	71	.438	40	.588	0	.000	51	111	24	12	48	7	91	182	3.2
Brown	68	671	78	.406	28	.609	1	.090	17	66	73	57	31	12	88	185	2.7

Chicago's Three Tenors. "Toni reluctantly bought into it," Jackson told *The New York Times*. "We asked him to be enthusiastic about it, not just accept it. That has been more difficult for him."

Even with Jackson's steady hand and Zen-like countenance, the 1995-96 Bulls couldn't be assured of anything, much less immortality. The road ahead seemed so long and littered with debris that 70 wins seemed as improbable as Jordan's return to his gravity-defying ways of the early '90s or an incident-free season from Rodman. "We realize," Pippen said in *The New York Times*, "that if we execute, we're going to beat every team in the league."

But would they execute?

* * * * * *

The journey began innocently enough. Yes, the Bulls bolted to a 10-2 start, but their two losses came to Orlando and Seattle, indicating that while the Bulls had superior firepower to subdue most of the league's teams (included in the 10 wins were road triumphs over San Antonio and Utah), they still weren't capable of stomping everybody every night.

"I think it was a good test," Jordan said after the 94-88 loss to a Shaqless (broken thumb) Orlando on November 14. "Now we see what we're dealing with. I think we have a better sense of (the Magic). We can make adjustments from here."

The 10-2 start was accomplished in typical Chicago fashion. Jordan was the supreme scorer, with Pippen the multitalented supporting star. Everybody else filled their roles. Rodman rebounded (and stayed out of trouble). Steve Kerr hit 3-pointers. Luc Longley banged around inside.

But it was Jordan's show, just like the old days. Because he had heard the accusations that his skills had diminished somewhat, Jordan came to training camp in tip-top shape

and with a vendetta against every person who questioned his status as the planet's best player.

"(The criticism) was a blessing because that was part of my motivation for this year," he told *Basketball America*. "Last year, I played 17 games, we get knocked out, and half the media guys say I lost a step and can't do the same things. That is motivation for me to go in the gym and lift weights and get my game back."

The early returns were stunning. In the 103-94 win at San Antonio November 22, Jordan tossed in 38 points. He was no less impressive elsewhere. When the Bulls were on the brink of a road humiliation in Vancouver on November 30, it was Jordan who went bonkers

Though relegated to the bench, Toni Kukoc wound up playing more minutes than starter Dennis Rodman and bedazzled opponents with his myriad offensive skills.

in the game's final six minutes, scoring 19 points to preserve a 94-88 win and showing the Canadians why they were right to beg for a spot in the greatest athletic show on Earth. Even his teammates were impressed. They serenaded him with Gatorade's "Be Like Mike" jingle following the outburst. Chicago closed November by winning seven of eight and had signaled to the league that its two-year hiatus from the winner's circle might just be over.

The opening act was great, yet it couldn't match what was to come.

On February 18, Scottie Pippen (40 points) and Michael Jordan (44) nearly outscored Indiana all by themselves. The Bulls won 110-102, avenging an earlier loss.

The Bulls rampaged through December 13-1, and the talk of 70 wins began to surface. The Bulls downplayed it, but it was clear they would need a period of substantial failure to amass the requisite losses that would prevent them from establishing the new record.

"I do not think 70 wins is something that we want to focus on this early in the season," Pippen said. "The thing about the NBA season is keeping guys healthy and maintaining the same effort every night. I think we are going to take one game at a time and just keep improving our record."

Chicago followed that game plan perfectly during the last month of 1995. On December 8, Rodman got his first shot at the Spurs (he had missed the first game in San Antonio), who had been telling anybody with a tape recorder just how happy they were to be without the human canvas. All Dennis the Menace did was grab 21 rebounds in a 106-87 rout at the United Center. The next night, in Milwaukee, it was Jordan's turn to shine. He scored 45 points to key a 118-106 win.

The Bulls gained a measure of revenge over Orlando on December 13 with a 112-103 win, preserving their perfect home record (9-0) and giving cable station TBS its highest rated NBA game ever. Even though the Magic were again playing without O'Neal, the win was a good one for the Bulls, who needed to make a statement against the team that had eliminated them from playoff contention the previous year.

The winning streak swelled to nine games three nights later, when Pippen, more comfortable now in his role as No. 2 option, scored 33 points and grabbed 13 boards in a 108-88 win over the Lakers.

"(Jordan's absence) made me realize how much I missed him when he was away," Pippen said. "I think his being out on the court definitely strengthens and enhances my game, because it gives me more opportunities. Having Michael out on the court takes some of the pressure off."

The rest of December was a red-and-black tidal wave through the NBA. On the 18th, Pippen and Jordan each had 37 in a 123-114 win at Boston. Three games later, Jordan had 30 and Pippen added 28 in a 100-86 win over Utah in Chicago. With the Bulls 23-2 on Christmas Day, it was clear a run at 70 was not at all a fantasy. And all that talk about the Bulls needing an entire season to blend their talents and personalities together was over-blown. The team had hit its stride quickly.

"I think this team is pretty mature," Jordan told *Basketball America*. "Phil Jackson is good at that, getting everyone prepared and keeping them focused. If you miss a player, you try to compensate and other players step up. I think that has been a strong point for this team."

Things would only get better during a 14-0 January. It was only the ninth perfect month in league history, and it kept the Bulls hot on the trail of the 1971-72 Lakers and the magical 70-win mark.

One of the highlights of the big month came January 13, when the Bulls' caravan pulled into Philadelphia for what was considered by many a meaningless walkover against the dreadful 76ers. But Sixers rookie Jerry Stackhouse had provided a subplot. The former North Carolina standout, who had left school two years early, was being hyped as the next Jordan. Stackhouse had even gone as far as to say that he didn't think anyone—including Jordan—could check him one-on-one.

To the hypercompetitive Jordan, it was more than a challenge. It was an insult. So, he hung up a workmanlike 48 points in the 120-93 win, leading Stackhouse to be appropriately contrite after the game. The rest of the month pretty much followed form. Jordan had 36 in a 111-96 win over Detroit. He posted 31, and Rodman contributed 20 rebounds, as the Bulls whipped Phoenix 93-82 for a franchise-record 15th straight victory.

As the victory total grew, so did the hysteria. The Bulls were no longer just a basketball team. They were a bona fide happening on hardwood and received rock-star treatment everywhere they went. Even reserves like Bill Wennington found fans waiting for him after games, hoping for an autograph or picture. "Sometimes *I* don't even wait for me," Wennington told *Esquire*.

Many felt that Dennis Rodman would never fit in with superstars Michael Jordan and Scottie Pippen, but it worked. "I love having Dennis around," Jordan said. "It's interesting and it's fun."

Comedian and basketball junkie Bill Murray (eating popcorn) as well as ESPN anchor Dan Patrick (to Murray's left) were among the many celebrities who visited the United Center.

In a practice previously reserved for rock stars, Dennis Rodman started giving away his jersey after games. He usually tossed it to a kid.

The Bulls became familiar with service elevators in every hotel and were forced to check in under assumed names. The focus of the mania remained the team's three-man nucleus—Superman, Batman, and Rodman. At the Los Angeles Forum on February 2, a man wearing a Bulls No. 23 jersey ran out of the stands while Jordan shot free throws during warmups and dove at Michael's feet, crying. Police had to escort him away. That game was a celebrity circus, as it pitted Michael vs. Magic Johnson, who days earlier had unretired and rejoined the Lakers. The Bulls prevailed 99-84 for their 18th straight victory.

Rodman, who cultivated his image with his lifestyle and attire, was even more in the spotlight because he didn't avoid it. He was accessible in restaurants and clubs and created a furor by giving away his jersey after games. When a local company painted a mural of him on a downtown building—complete with changing hair hues—it created such a distraction among motorists on a nearby highway that the thing had to be removed in the name of a peaceful commute to work. In a sport that has ballooned because of shrewd marketing, the Bulls were

clearly the most valuable—and popular—commodity.

"It's like pictures of the Kennedy funeral, the motorcade," Erik Helland, the team's strength and conditioning coach, told *The New York Times Magazine*. "You see all these reactions from adults you wouldn't normally see—the people pointing, mouths open."

Once the fabulous January was completed, the debate about whether the Bulls could win 70 reached a fever pitch. Nearly every media outlet was covering the Chicago charge in some way or another, and the league's principles were debating whether the team's torrid 41-3 start—a league record for most wins with just three losses—would continue through the final two-plus months of the regular season.

While the players went about the daily business of chasing the magical mark, they appeared to keep their minds on the ultimate goal. Yes, the ride had been fun to this point, but the final destination lay well beyond the 70-win mark.

"This season has been enjoyable for a lot of us, especially the guys who have never experienced what we are experiencing now," said Jordan, who would go on to win the

SEASON HIGHLIGHTS

- **December 8** Squaring off against his old San Antonio teammates, Dennis Rodman pulls down 21 boards in a 106-87 romp, giving coach Phil Jackson a franchise-record 357 victories.

- **December 23** Chicago dusts off Utah 100-86 for its 13th straight victory and a 23-2 record.

- **January 13** Jordan outscores cocky rookie Jerry Stackhouse 48-13, as the Bulls deep-six the 76ers 120-93 and improve to 30-3.

- **February 2** Stars pack the L.A. Forum to see Jordan face the comebacking Magic Johnson. The Bulls prevail 99-84 for their 18th straight victory and ninth straight road win (both team records) and improve to 41-3.

- **February 18** The Bulls beat Indiana 110-102 as Jordan scores 44 and Scottie Pippen pockets 40.

- **February 27** Rodman grabs 24 rebounds as the Bulls maul Minnesota 120-99. Chicago reaches 50 wins (50-6) faster than any team in major-sports history.

- **March 7** Outballoted by Grant Hill in All-Star voting, Jordan burns Hill's Pistons for 53 points as Chicago knocks off Detroit 102-81.

- **April 4** The Bulls extend their home winning streak to 44—an NBA record—with a 100-92 triumph over Miami.

- **April 14** Chicago knocks off Cleveland 98-72 to tie the 1971-72 Lakers for most wins in a season (69).

- **April 16** Despite 39-percent field-goal shooting, the Bulls win at Milwaukee 86-80 for their NBA-record 70th victory.

Opposite page: The Bulls' victory in Orlando proved they could win in the NBA's toughest building (the United Center notwithstanding). Above left: Once seen as a me-first scorer, Ron Harper transformed into a team-first role player. Above right: Steve Kerr shot 3-pointers at a 51.5-percent clip.

NBA scoring championship with 30.4 points per game. "(Winning 70 games) has given us something to drive for. . . . But we don't want to get so concentrated on the 70 games and forget what our ultimate purpose is, which is to win a championship."

Chicago's 18-game winning streak came to an end on the road, with consecutive losses to Denver (105-99) and Phoenix (106-96) in early February. Even though Jordan

scored 39 against the Nuggets, he did so on 13-of-29 shooting. Meanwhile, Denver guard Mahmoud Abdul-Rauf erupted for 32 and added nine assists. Two nights later against the Suns, Kevin Johnson had 20 points and 10 assists in the 10-point win, which prompted Suns star Charles Barkley to issue a warning to the Bulls.

"They are not going to be handed the championship," Barkley said. "Orlando and Indiana can beat them, and there are teams out west that can beat them. They will win a lot of games in the regular season . . . but they are going to have some tough series in the playoffs."

Neither Barkley's admonition nor the two losses seemed to shake Chicago, which won 13 of its next 14 games—often in spectacular style. In a 110-102 win at Indiana

on February 18, Jordan (44 points) and Pippen (40) became just the ninth pair of teammates (and only the sixth in a nonovertime game) to score 40 or more in the same game. Just for good measure, Rodman contributed 23 rebounds.

March featured an inevitable slowing of the pace. Pippen missed a stretch of games with injuries, as did center Luc Longley. And the Bulls actually lost to the expansion Toronto Raptors, 109-108. Though 70 wins seemed well within reason (the Bulls finished the month 62-8), the big news was the long-awaited Rodman Detonation.

It came in a 97-93 road win in New Jersey, the kind of desultory contest that barely warrants mention in the national headlines. But Rodman made sure Chicago would be right up on top when he head-

ruary 23 loss in south Florida. Three days later, the Bulls whipped host Orlando 90-86, sending a loud and clear playoff message. Next up was a spot in the history books.

The Magic Moment came April 16 in Milwaukee. As the Bulls headed north by bus to the Bradley Center, fans waved from overpasses along the Tri-State Expressway. Toll-takers snapped pictures. "Not a normal day at all," Jackson said.

There was nothing overly spectacular about the game, an 86-80 win. Longley had 16 points and seven rebounds and drained a pair of key free throws with 21.9 seconds remaining that all but sealed the win. A Jordan block of a Johnny Newman 3-pointer seven seconds later provided a fitting punctuation mark on the win and the record.

"This is going to take some time to sink in," Jordan said afterward in the Bulls' relatively subdued locker room. "After so many things I've done, after the national championships and the NBA titles and gold medals, it's too early to compare this."

The Bulls claimed victory No. 72 in Washington on the last day of the season. Chicago's dominance was reflected in the numbers. The Bulls led the league in scoring (105.2 points per game), scoring differential (+12.2 per game), and rebounding differential (+6.6 per game) and were among the best in the league in virtually every other statistical category.

But it wasn't as easy as you'd think.

"You don't know about the pressure we have to deal with every night to play the game of basketball," Jordan said. "As much as you might say we have too many expansion teams and the league is diluted, you can also say there's a lot of distractions around now. The way we look at it is that we went out and put forth the effort and got 70 wins."

Plus two.

Top: *Celtics fans had seen green for many years, but never on a player's head. Dennis Rodman went with this look during the Christmas season.* Bottom: *Jerry Krause had taken gambles drafting Scottie Pippen (tiny school) and Toni Kukoc (Europe) as well as signing Rodman, but in each case he hit the jackpot.*

butted referee Ted Bernhardt after receiving two technical fouls. On his way off the court, Rodman kayoed a bucket of Gatorade, just for good measure. It was an over-the-top performance, even for Rodman, and the league office responded with a six-game suspension.

The outburst had little effect, other than to serve notice that Rodman remained the league's most volatile and unpredictable source. Jordan scored 38 two nights later in a surprisingly tough 98-94 win in Philadelphia. Michael then lifted the Bulls to an 89-67 triumph over Sacramento that was Chicago's 40th straight home win.

April dawned with the Bulls back at full strength and 70 wins all but guaranteed. Pippen was back healthy. Rodman had served his time. And Jordan was just Jordan. On April 4, he scored 40 points in a 100-92 win over Miami that avenged a Feb-

BULLS' GAME-BY-GAME RESULTS

Date		Opponent	Score	Date		Opponent	Score
November 3	vs.	Charlotte	105-91	February 22	at	Atlanta	96-91
November 4	vs.	Boston	107-85	**February 23**	**at**	**Miami**	**104-113**
November 7	vs.	Toronto	117-108	February 25	vs.	Orlando	111-91
November 9	at	Cleveland	106-88	February 27	vs.	Minnesota	120-99
November 11	vs.	Portland	110-106	March 1	vs.	Golden State	110-87
November 14	**at**	**Orlando**	**88-94**	March 2	vs.	Boston	107-75
November 15	vs.	Cleveland	113-94	March 5	vs.	Milwaukee	115-106
November 17	vs.	New Jersey	109-94	March 7	vs.	Detroit	102-81
November 21	at	Dallas	108-102	**March 10**	**at**	**New York**	**72-104**
November 22	at	San Antonio	103-94	March 13	vs.	Washington	103-86
November 24	at	Utah	90-85	March 15	vs.	Denver	108-87
November 26	**at**	**Seattle**	**92-97**	March 16	at	New Jersey	97-93
November 27	at	Portland	107-104	March 18	at	Philadelphia	98-94
November 30	at	Vancouver	94-88	March 19	vs.	Sacramento	89-67
December 2	at	L.A. Clippers	104-98	March 21	vs.	New York	107-86
December 6	vs.	New York	101-94	**March 24**	**at**	**Toronto**	**108-109**
December 8	vs.	San Antonio	106-87	March 28	vs.	Atlanta	111-80
December 9	at	Milwaukee	118-106	March 30	vs.	L.A. Clippers	106-85
December 13	vs.	Orlando	112-103	April 2	at	Miami	110-92
December 14	at	Atlanta	127-108	April 4	vs.	Miami	100-92
December 16	vs.	L.A. Lakers	108-88	April 5	at	Charlotte	126-92
December 18	at	Boston	123-114	April 7	at	Orlando	90-86
December 19	vs.	Dallas	114-101	**April 8**	**vs.**	**Charlotte**	**97-98**
December 22	vs.	Toronto	113-104	April 11	at	New Jersey	113-100
December 23	vs.	Utah	100-86	April 12	vs.	Philadelphia	112-82
December 26	**at**	**Indiana**	**97-103**	April 14	at	Cleveland	98-72
December 29	vs.	Indiana	120-93	April 16	at	Milwaukee	86-80
December 30	vs.	Atlanta	95-93	April 18	vs.	Detroit	110-79
January 3	vs.	Houston	100-86	**April 20**	**vs.**	**Indiana**	**99-100**
January 4	at	Charlotte	117-93	April 21	at	Washington	103-93
January 6	vs.	Milwaukee	113-84				
January 10	vs.	Seattle	113-87				
January 13	at	Philadelphia	120-93				
January 15	at	Washington	116-109				
January 16	vs.	Philadelphia	116-104				
January 18	at	Toronto	92-89				
January 21	at	Detroit	111-96				
January 23	at	New York	99-79				
January 24	vs.	Vancouver	104-84				
January 26	vs.	Miami	102-80				
January 28	vs.	Phoenix	93-82				
January 30	at	Houston	98-87				
February 1	at	Sacramento	105-85				
February 2	at	L.A. Lakers	99-84				
February 4	**at**	**Denver**	**99-105**				
February 6	**at**	**Phoenix**	**96-106**				
February 7	at	Golden State	99-95				
February 13	vs.	Washington	111-98				
February 15	at	Detroit	112-109				
February 16	at	Minnesota	103-100				
February 18	at	Indiana	110-102				
February 20	vs.	Cleveland	102-76				

Note: Bulls' losses in red.

This victory in Milwaukee gave the Bulls victory No. 70, the number fans had been pointing to since January.

COOL AIR

With the pressures of the world on his shoulders, how does Michael Jordan remain so calm and collected?

Asked once to describe himself, Michael Jordan said: "He's a fun-loving person. He smiles, he's outgoing, and he tries to be the best he can at whatever he does. He feels like he's a role model for kids, and I would say he's good-looking." With that, Jordan let loose a grin: "But that might be saying too much."

Cool. Very cool.

The most phenomenal thing about Michael Jordan is that he does it all, and does it all so well. And that doesn't mean just on the court, where he scores, passes, rebounds, defends, leads, teaches, and hits the winning shot at the buzzer. He does it all off the court, too. He's a husband, father of three, business owner, charity worker, actor, corporate sponsor, golfer, author, and role model. And despite the money-minded who claw and scratch for his time—as well as the screaming throngs of fans—Jordan remains cool and composed. Humble and polite. Even charming.

So how does he pull it off? To find the answer, one must dig deep into his past, to Wilmington, North Carolina, to the backyard of the Jordan family home. It was Michael's mother and father who taught him early the virtues of courtesy, honesty, and the respect of elders.

Above: *Michael said his personality and sense of humor came from his father, the late James Jordan.* **Right:** *Though eliminated by Orlando in the 1995 playoffs, Jordan showed he still had the magic in 1996.*

"My family has been my inspiration to succeed," Jordan said. "My childhood means a lot to me. They were pushing me and fighting with me and helping me become the man I am today. My personality and my laughter come from my father. My business and serious side come from my mother."

Deloris Jordan said her fourth child showed more of her father's personality when he was small. "He was such a jolly baby," she said. "He never cried. Just feed him and give him something to play with,

and he was fine. He doesn't like sadness. He gets very quiet around that. Once, a girlfriend of his drowned when he was in college. He took it very badly. He wants to make it right, no matter what it is. He doesn't want problems. He wants everybody to be happy."

As most children do, Michael also had his mischievous side. "You had to discipline him," Deloris said. "He would test you to the limit. Michael was always getting into things."

Michael was also, in his words, "gooney," and he so feared that no

THE JORDAN FILE

Position: Guard
Height: 6'6" **Weight:** 216
Birth date: February 17, 1963
NBA Experience: 11 years
College: North Carolina
Acquired: 1st-round pick in 1984 draft (3rd overall)

CAREER HIGHLIGHTS

- Holds NBA records for highest career scoring average in the regular season, playoffs, and All-Star Games
- Eight-time NBA scoring champion (1986-87 through 1992-93 1995-96)
- Four-time NBA Most Valuable Player (1987-88, 1990-91, 1991-92, and 1995-96)
- Winner of three straight NBA Finals Most Valuable Player Awards (1991 through 1993)
- NBA Rookie of the Year in 1984-85
- NBA Defensive Player of the Year in 1987-88
- Two-time Olympic gold medalist (1984 and 1992)
- NCAA champion in 1982
- College Player of the Year in 1983-84

After a young Michael showed he could climb the sky with his Air Jordans, every boy who could dribble wanted to buy his shoes.

one would want to marry him that he took a home-economics course in school. He learned how to cook, sew, and clean. "I remember he baked a cake in school that was so good, we couldn't believe it," Deloris said. "We had to call his teacher to verify it."

One thing Michael wasn't very good at was working. "Michael is probably the laziest kid I had," said his late father, James, who grew up the son of a poor farmer and was driving a tractor by the age of 10. "If he had to get a job in a factory punching a clock, he'd starve to death. He would give every last dime of his allowance to his brothers and sisters and even kids in the neighborhood to do his chores. He was always broke."

Somehow, James the father was able to impart to his son Michael a feeling of being grateful for what he had. Listen closely to the father, and remember when you hear it from the son.

"Deloris and I grew up among whites and got along," said James, who died in 1993. "It's not really what color you are, it's who you are. It's not what you amass or have that makes you different, it's your personality. You can have the most money in the world and still be a jerk. You can have no money at all and be the nicest man in the world. People who like you for what you are, those are your real friends. We made sure they understood that lesson. None of my kids were ever touched by segregation."

"That's the greatest lesson I've learned from my parents," Michael said. "I never see you for the color. I see you for the person you are. I know I'm recognized as being black, but I don't look at you as black or white, just as a person. I think one of the reasons I've been accepted by people of so many different races is that my personality fits that. I grew up with David Bridges, who is white, since we were five years old, and we're still very close. I roomed with Buzz Peterson [who is white] in college."

Michael is more comfortable and trusting with those who knew and liked him from before than the Johnny-come-latelies who are clutching onto a piece of him in his ever-ascending stardom. When Jordan arrived in Chicago, he struck up a friendship with George Koehler, his white limousine driver. They practically lived together before Jordan got married. When it became impractical for Michael to stop in and purchase one of his culinary favorites, Kentucky Fried Chicken, it was always Koehler who would make the run. Jordan came to rely on him for all the little things in life as well as the companionship of a good friend.

Growing up in Wilmington, Michael was closest to his older

brother by a year, Larry. The ferocity of their backyard one-on-one games has taken on near-legendary proportions. Talk about blood, sweat, and tears; their confrontations were the epitome of competitiveness. Larry, at 5'8", was actually a greater leaper than the famed Air Jordan. For the longest time, Larry was a better player, usually getting the best of his little brother in these sibling showdowns. "Oh yeah, I used to be able to take him most of the time," said Larry, who competed for

> **"I remember [Michael] baked a cake in school that was so good, we couldn't believe it. We had to call his teacher to verify it."**
> **—Deloris Jordan**

one season in the World Basketball League for players 6'4" and under, dunking two-handed, backwards, with ease. "But once he began shooting up and getting taller, I had more trouble staying with him."

"Those backyard games really helped me become the player I am today in a lot of ways," Michael said. "Larry would never give me any slack, never took it easy on me. He'd rather beat me up than have me beat him in a game. I learned a lot about being competitive from him."

James Jordan moved his family to Wilmington when Michael was age

When Jordan announced he was going to North Carolina, friends told him he'd never get off the bench. As a junior, he was named College Player of the Year.

seven. Besides Larry, there is the oldest son, James Ronald, and sisters Delois and Roslyn. James told the *Chicago Tribune:* "Four of my kids have done well in life; one has done overly well. He finds it in his heart to share."

"I never want them to feel that they're not a part of my success," Michael told the *Tribune.* "My parents, brothers, and sisters are very prideful people. They like to work for their own things. I have to actually make them accept some things I want them to have. Still, I'm willing to help them in any way possible."

A few years ago, James Jordan looked back on how he raised Michael. He smiled and shook his head. "In as much as Michael learned a lot growing up, Deloris and I learned a lot as he grew up," he said. "All that has happened, I had no idea. Maybe it's better. If I had, I might've pushed him too hard and screwed him up. As it was, everything happened very naturally. Here's a kid who grew up with nothing and always had to work to make ends meet. He came out of a city where they never recruited a player. I look at it, think about it quite often.

"I've got to believe one thing. One day, God was sitting around and decided to make himself the perfect basketball player. He gave him a little hardship early in life to make him appreciate what he would earn in the end, and called him Michael Jordan."

* * * * * *

Michael Jordan wasn't born a basketball phenom and wasn't a prodigy like Isiah Thomas, who

competed with 13-year-olds when he was seven. No, Jordan didn't become intensely serious about basketball until he was a sophomore at Laney High School in Wilmington. He averaged 25 points a game with the junior-varsity team that season, only to have his ego bruised when another player was promoted to the varsity ahead of him.

Jordan's response was to work relentlessly on his game during the summer. Even his beloved baseball took a back seat. As a junior, he not only made the varsity team, he averaged 20 points a game. That grew to 23 points a game his senior year.

"He could do more things than the average high school player," recalled Ruby Sutton, Laney's volleyball and boys tennis coach. "Still, he was a normal student. Because he was good at what he did, that didn't make him a conceited person. And yes, he stuck his tongue out even back then."

Jordan proceeded to the University of North Carolina because of his admiration and respect for venerable coach Dean Smith. "You'll never play there," friends and advisors warned Michael. But Jordan already was busting loose. He played 34 games as a freshman, averaging 13.5 points and 4.4 rebounds while shooting 53.4 percent. At the time, he was one of eight freshmen ever to start for Smith, who favors the gradual development of his recruits.

There have been many glorious moments in the history of North Carolina basketball. But if you ask Tar Heel fans for the most memorable, they'll tell you about the NCAA championship game in 1982 when the freshman Jordan stepped up and hit the game-winning shot. That was no ordinary freshman, of course, yet we're talk-

Jordan goes hard to the hoop against Cleveland's Craig Ehlo, who fouls Michael in desperation. Against the Cavaliers in the 1988 playoffs, Jordan had games of 50, 55, 38, 44, and 39 points.

> **"That's where we put the ball in his hands and say, 'Save us, Michael.'"**
> **—John Bach on the Archangel Offense**

ing about a kid who had just turned 19 making a shot that had huge ramifications for the program.

Smith had been to the Final Four before but hadn't won it. In 1977, it was widely acknowledged that he had the best team in the country, but injuries to Phil Ford, Tom La-Garde, and Walter Davis left the Tar Heels subpar and unable to beat Marquette for the title. In 1981, one of the best units again resided in Chapel Hill. This time, it lost to Indiana in the finals.

So Smith's reputation was on the line that night in 1982. George-

With their famed Jordan Rules— which included double-teaming Michael before he even got the ball—the Detroit Pistons became the first team to corral Jordan.

town, with the fearsome Patrick Ewing, led 62-61 with 31 seconds left when Smith signaled for a time-out. He sat his starting five—Jordan, James Worthy, Sam Perkins, Jimmy Black, Matt Doherty—and mapped strategy. The first option was to work the ball inside to Worthy or Perkins. Yet Smith sensed something else was about to unfold. As the Tar Heels broke their huddle, he turned to Jordan and said: "Do it, Michael. Just knock it in."

Sure enough, Ewing closed down the inside, discouraging the Carolina passers from executing their prime directive. Eventually, they swung the ball to Jordan. The moment is captured on film, forever being replayed during March Madness. He was 16 feet away from the basket on the left wing and there were 15 seconds showing on the clock. He unleashed his fateful jumper.

Michael's father covered his face, afraid to watch what destiny had in store for his fourth child. How did he find out what happened? "I knew from Deloris," James said. "She said something you can't repeat in a newspaper. She screamed: 'Holy (barnyard expletive), he made it!'"

* * * * * *

Fast-forward to 1989 and the final game of a hotly contested playoff series between Jordan's Bulls and the Cleveland Cavaliers. Cleveland led 100-99 with three seconds remaining. The Bulls had the ball, and every one of the 20,000 fans at Richfield Coliseum knew where it was going. Bulls assistant coach John Bach had long ago nicknamed this the "Archangel Offense." Said Bach: "That's where we put the ball in his hands and say, 'Save us, Michael.'"

It had taken seven years for Michael to give Chicago its first-ever NBA title. Jordan broke into tears after defeating the Lakers in the 1991 NBA Finals.

Jordan broke to the inbound pass with Larry Nance and Craig Ehlo in hot pursuit. Ehlo was Jordan's defender, and Nance simply abandoned his assignment—so intent was he on stopping Jordan. Michael got the ball, pivoted, took a dribble past Nance, and took off from the right of the free-throw line. Jordan pumped once as he drifted to the left, freeing himself from Ehlo, who appeared to give Jordan a little nudge. Still gliding, Jordan shot the ball at the basket. It was the same sensation as hitting a moving target. Somehow, Jordan swished the 15-footer for a 101-100 victory. He landed on both feet, leaped into the air, and pumped his fist once. Teammates mobbed him.

The repercussions of that shot are still being felt. Frustrated and upset at being eliminated by a Bulls team they considered inferior, Cleveland management made changes. Ron

Harper (a current Bull) was dealt to the L.A. Clippers for Danny Ferry. The Cavaliers haven't been NBA contenders since. For the Bulls, the shot was a springboard to greatness in the 1990s.

* * * * * *

Jordan's heroics against Georgetown and Cleveland are two of dozens of examples of him coming through when the chips were down. "Jordan usually saves his best stuff for the playoffs," wrote *The New York Times,* "when the stakes are highest, when the pressure is greatest and when lesser teams fold."

Ironically, the Bulls were one of those lesser teams during Jordan's early years in the NBA. Those were the days when the Bulls were known as "Michael and the Jordanaires." Orlando Woolridge might have been the only other legitimate player. Jordan was surrounded by a motley cast that included Dave Corzine, Caldwell Jones, Jawann Oldham, Sidney Green, Steve Johnson, Wes Matthews, Ennis Whatley, Rod Higgins, and David Greenwood.

Julius Erving and other stars told the brilliant newcomer to pace

himself, not to burn out like a supernova. Jordan would listen thoughtfully, then a frown would crinkle up his forehead. How do you go about pacing yourself? Does that mean you don't go all-out on every play? It was inconceivable to a guy who loved playing so much that he had a "Love of the Game" clause inserted into his contract, allowing him to play in pickup games whenever he wanted.

Larry Bird became a Jordan believer during an early meeting in which Jordan had 41 points, 12 rebounds, and seven assists. "Unlike anyone I've ever seen," Bird said. "Phenomenal. One of a kind. He's the best. Ever."

Even better than Larry Bird? "Yup. At this stage in his career, he's doing more than I ever did. I couldn't do what he did as a rookie. Heck, there was one drive tonight: He had the ball up in his right hand, then he took it down, then he brought it back up. I got a hand on it, fouled him, and he still scored. And all the while he's in the air. You have to play this game to know how difficult that is. You see that and figure, 'Well, what the heck can you do?'"

Jordan averaged more than 28 points a game his first season,

In one of the rare public gatherings of the whole Jordan clan, Michael is pictured with wife Juanita, daughter Jasmine, and sons Marcus and Jeffrey (far right).

Michael skies hoopward in the 1991 NBA Finals. Jordan averaged 31.2 points and 11.4 assists in the series and was named Finals MVP.

1984-85, and was named Rookie of the Year. As hard as it is to believe now, Chicago Stadium was more than half empty some nights, as the Bulls finished 38-44. They did, however, make the playoffs for the first time in four years.

Jordan's second season began with a broken foot (he missed 64 games) and ended with the greatest scoring outburst in NBA playoff history: 63 points in a 135-

> ❝**Unlike anyone I've ever seen. Phenomenal. One of a kind. He's the best. Ever.**❞
> —**Larry Bird**

131 double-overtime loss to the Celtics. In one memorable sequence, he dribbled between his legs and then around Bird. He shot by Dennis Johnson, took off over Kevin McHale, and double-pumped a layup with Robert Parish flailing away. One against four and Jordan won.

Jordan's first coach with the Bulls, Kevin Loughery, said he'll never forget one night in the 1984-85 season when Jordan appeared to be walking on air. "We were playing the Bullets in Washington," Loughery said. "And you got to understand: Michael's first year, we had him, Orlando Woolridge, and not much else. Anyway, Michael's driving toward the circle and begins taking off at the top of the key. He looks to his left and spots Ennis Whatley open, except Ennis couldn't hit a

Mike poses with Mick on Walt Disney World's Osprey Ridge golf course. At one point, Jordan had hoped to play on the PGA Tour after retiring from basketball.

jump shot that night to save his life. So, [Michael] glances to his right and there's Wes Matthews, who isn't shooting much better than Ennis. Still in the air, Michael takes one last look back at Ennis, then double-pumps and banks it in. That's the most amazing thing I've ever seen."

In the 1986-87 season, his third in the league, Jordan became the first player in 24 years to crack the 3,000-point barrier. His average of 37.1 points led the league and began a run of seven consecutive scoring titles. He accomplished this in the face of double- and triple-teaming defenses and other "anti-Air" gimmicks designed to stop him. He opened the season with 50 points, and he later had games of 50, 53, 53, 56, 58, 61, and 61. He scored an NBA-record 23 consecutive points in one game, and he scored 40 or more points in nine straight games (that hadn't happened in the NBA in 24 years).

"In all my basketball fantasies over the years," said Hall of Famer Rick Barry, "I never dreamed the things Michael Jordan actually does."

To the astonishment of some, Jordan didn't win the NBA Most Valuable Player Award that season. It was easy for detractors to dismiss him as a gunner, while extolling the virtues of Bird and Magic Johnson (the 1986-87 winner), both three-time MVPs and catalysts on perennial championship contenders. Nonsense, said Chicago coach Doug Collins. "The Bulls without Michael Jordan would be the L.A. Clippers."

> **❝Magic and Bird are the best players in the game who play on the floor. Michael is the best player in the game who plays in the air.❞**
> **—John Paxson**

"Magic and Bird are the best players in the game who play on the floor," said former Bulls guard John Paxson. "Michael is the best player in the game who plays in the air."

Jordan was untouchable in his fourth season, 1987-88, and finally won the MVP Award. In a league full of thoroughbreds, he was Secretariat. He became the first player in NBA history to win the scoring title (35.0 points a game) and be named Defensive Player of the Year in the same season. He led the league in steals (3.16 a game), blocked more shots than 16 starting centers, won the NBA's Slam Dunk Contest, and became the only player ever to block 100 shots and record 200 steals in consecutive seasons. He also reached four NBA and eight club playoff records.

"Jordan single-handedly dismembered and dismantled all of us," said Boston's Kevin McHale after a 50-point outburst by Michael. Then there was the night he torched Cleveland's Craig Ehlo for 52. "I was handed my breakfast, lunch, and dinner all in one night," sighed Ehlo.

Jordan wasn't through torturing Ehlo. Not even close. Jordan had a career series in leading the Bulls past Cleveland in the 1988 playoffs. He had 50 points in the opener. After burning Ehlo again, Jordan heard Cavs guard Ron Harper say that Michael would "never get 50 on me." So in Game 2, Jordan against Harper, Jordan scored 55. He was the first guy ever to do the 50-50 thing in successive postseason games. (Between games, he shot a 75 at a Chicago-area golf course.)

Jordan had "only" 38 points and nine assists in a loss in Game 3 and 44 when the Cavaliers evened the series. He had 39 in the decisive win back home. Jordan finished the series averaging an absurd 45.2 points a game, a record for a five-game series.

Next were the Detroit Pistons, against whom Jordan had scored 59 points in the regular season, a performance that may have been the motivation for Detroit to develop what later came to be known as the "Jordan Rules." Devised by Detroit assistant coach Ron Rothstein, the Jordan Rules encompassed 13 defensive sets to counter Jordan's favorite and most effective moves. What the Jordan Rules boil down to is that the Pistons double-teamed him before he got the ball, and when that wasn't possible, they forced him one way into a double-

Though he averaged just 14.9 points per game for the 1992 Olympic Dream Team (second on the squad behind Charles Barkley's 18.0), Jordan scored a team-high 22 in the gold-medal game victory over Croatia.

team trap. The strategy worked beautifully as the Pistons knocked out the Bulls in five games.

Detroit would bounce the Bulls from the playoffs again the following spring, 1989, after a regular season in which Jordan reached

In the critical Game 5 of the 1992 NBA Finals, Jordan burned the Trail Blazers for 46 points as the Bulls won 119-106.

10,000 career points faster than anyone but Wilt Chamberlain. Collins experimented with Michael at point guard for awhile, and he responded with triple-doubles in seven consecutive games.

Collins coached Jordan for three years before being fired in 1989. "There is nothing Michael can't do," he told Knight-Ridder's Ray Didinger. "I love Dennis Rodman, but Michael plays tougher defense than Dennis.

If you polled the NBA guards and asked them to pick the one man they'd least like to have guard them in the last 24 seconds of a game, I'll bet most of them would pick Michael. And if you asked them to pick the one player they would least like to defend in the last 24 seconds, it would be Michael by a landslide. That's a pretty nice compliment. In crunch time, this one guy is the best at both ends of the floor. I don't know if there's ever been another player like that."

Phil Jackson replaced Collins as coach for the 1989-90 season, and it was onward and upward for the Bulls. They lost to Detroit again in the 1990 playoffs, this time in seven games in the Eastern Conference finals, then reeled off three consecutive championships, defeating the Los Angeles Lakers, the Portland Trail Blazers, and the Phoenix Suns.

One moment etched in basketball lore came in Game 1 of the Portland series, just after Jordan had hit a record sixth 3-pointer in the first half of the Bulls' victory. As he was "Cadillacing" back up-court in his easy gait, Jordan turned toward a TV camera and shrugged his shoulders, both hands uplifted, as if to express: "What can I say?"

"It was beautiful," Magic Johnson said of the Portland series and Jordan's MVP performance. "I don't think people understand or realize that when you talk about a Larry Bird or a Michael Jordan, you won't be getting these guys anymore. It's hard to come up with guys like Michael. Fans have got to realize, this is it. You've got to absorb all of it because when he's gone, there's not going to be any more Michael Jordans."

Winning the third title made the Bulls arguably the second-greatest NBA team of all time, trailing only the eight-time champion Boston Celtics of the 1960s. Having assured the Bulls' place in history and having carved his niche one rung higher than repeat NBA champs

JORDAN'S NBA REGULAR-SEASON STATISTICS

| | G | MIN | FGs | | 3-PT FGs | | FTs | | Rebounds | | AST | STL | BLK | PTS | PPG |
			FG	PCT	FG	PCT	FT	PCT	OFF	TOT					
1984-85 CHI	82	3144	837	.515	9	.173	630	.845	167	534	481	196	69	2313	28.2
1985-86 CHI	18	451	150	.457	3	.167	105	.840	23	64	53	37	21	408	22.7
1986-87 CHI	82	3281	1098	.482	12	.182	833	.857	166	430	377	236	125	3041	37.1
1987-88 CHI	82	3311	1069	.535	7	.132	723	.841	139	449	485	259	131	2868	35.0
1988-89 CHI	81	3255	966	.538	27	.276	674	.850	149	652	650	234	65	2633	32.5
1989-90 CHI	82	3197	1034	.526	92	.376	593	.848	143	565	519	227	54	2753	33.6
1990-91 CHI	82	3034	990	.539	29	.312	571	.851	118	492	453	223	83	2580	31.5
1991-92 CHI	80	3102	943	.519	27	.270	491	.832	91	511	489	182	75	2404	30.0
1992-93 CHI	78	3067	992	.495	81	.352	476	.837	135	522	428	221	61	2541	32.6
1994-95 CHI	17	668	166	.411	16	.500	109	.801	25	117	90	30	13	457	26.9
1995-96 CHI	82	3090	916	.495	111	.427	548	.834	148	543	352	180	42	2491	30.4
Totals	766	29600	9161	.512	414	.332	5751	.844	1304	4879	4377	2025	739	24489	32.0

Magic and Isiah Thomas and surpassing Bird—who never won two consecutive—Jordan could finally rest. On October 6, 1993, he announced he was retiring from professional basketball.

* * * * * *

"My favorite childhood memory, my greatest accomplishment, was when I got the Most Valuable Player award when my Babe Ruth League team won the state baseball championship," Jordan once said. "That

> **"My lifestyle is so positive that I'm not afraid of something from the past coming back to haunt me or upset the role-model image I've set. I live a clean, healthy life, and I'm happy about it."**
> **—Michael Jordan**

was the first big thing I accomplished in my life, and you always remember the first." Jordan claims to this day that he treasures that baseball championship even more than the NCAA title he helped bring to North Carolina in 1982 or the Olympic gold medal he earned two years later.

"The way he played baseball in Little League, he made me become a fan," Jordan's father said. "If I wouldn't take him to play ball, he'd look so pitiful, like he'd lost every friend in the world and was all by himself. You'd take one look at him and say, 'OK, let's go.' He would do things in baseball and excel beyond kids his age that you would just get caught up in it."

Yet to the surprise of almost everyone, Michael returned to baseball when he retired from the Bulls. It had been more than a dozen years since he had played in a competitive game. But there he was, daily taking batting practice and fielding practice in the basement of Chicago's Comiskey Park or at Illinois Institute of Technology. There were times when his batting practice was supervised by the White Sox's guru of hitting, batting coach

Walt Hriniak. Jordan was hitting 600 to 1,000 balls a day and studying tapes of hitters such as Frank Thomas. In February 1994, the White Sox signed him to a minor-league contract.

The skeptics immediately raised the roof. "A million-to-one shot," was the consensus among the commentators. Of course, those were odds that Jordan was willing to take. "He won't be able to take the 12-hour bus rides," the fans on call-in shows intoned. Michael was 6'6", and he was used to flying to games, so he went out and bought his team a more roomy bus. He was, after all, Michael Jordan.

There are no shortcuts to becoming a good hitter, Jordan told everyone as he donned his baseball gear early in the season. And as Mike Lum, the roving hitting instructor for the White Sox minor-league system, told *USA Today Baseball Weekly*, "I know a lot of people aren't taking [Michael] seriously, but if they could be around him and see his work ethic, they would change their minds. He is always out early for extra batting practice. He was on the field at 7:30 every morning during spring training. He wants to learn."

Jordan's fans, however, wanted only to see their hero up close. From spring training in Florida to

games with the Double-A Birmingham Bulls during the season to the Arizona Fall League for top prospects, enthusiastic fans filled stands and cheered Jordan's every move. The Birmingham franchise and other teams in the Southern League broke attendance records, and some say that Jordan's presence might have preserved the Arizona Fall League's existence.

Michael was present, however, only to become a professional baseball player. His raw numbers for his lone season at Double-A don't jump out at you. He batted .202 with three homers and 51 runs batted in in 436 at-bats. But a closer look reveals that he was becoming a real prospect. He batted .260 in the last four weeks of the season, and he totaled 30 stolen bases, good for fifth in the Southern League. While with baseball's top prospects, Michael made another stride, batting .252. All agreed that it was amazing for anyone who hadn't played baseball in a dozen years to come into pro ball and compete right away at such a high level. It wasn't just anyone who did it, however. It was Michael Jordan.

As did other minor-leaguers in 1995, Jordan reported to spring training anxious to renew his bid to become a major-league player. He thought that this was to be his breakthrough season. Michael was in all likelihood going to report to Triple-A Nashville after spring training. Many experts thought that if he continued to make the same kind of progress that he did while he was a Double-A player, he would get a call-up in September, if not sooner. There was a new obstacle in Michael's way, however: the strike.

Major-league players had gone on strike in August 1994, and there was no break in the negotiations.

Jordan set an NBA Finals record by averaging 41.0 points a game during the 1993 series against Phoenix. Included were 55 in Game 4.

The Bulls retired Michael's No. 23 after his retirement in 1993. Jordan switched to No. 45 upon his comeback in 1994-95, then donned No. 23 again in 1995-96.

Jordan refused to comment on the overall labor situation, preferring to concentrate on the aspects of his game that he needed to improve. He also knew that anything that he said might come back to haunt him.

In March, White Sox general manager Ron Schueler told those White Sox minor-leaguers who refused to participate as "replacement players" to move their gear from the major-league clubhouse to the minor-league facility. Michael packed his gear and moved it to his car. His baseball career was over.

* * * * * *

To his infinite credit, Michael takes this role-model stuff seriously. Meanwhile, the public's love affair with him grows more passionate with every game. Kids and grown-ups alike sense a certain humility about him, that he doesn't feel he's any better than the next man and, personality-wise at least, can fit right in with the common folks. And they admire him because he doesn't do drugs.

Said Michael: "My lifestyle is so positive that I'm not afraid of something from the past coming back to haunt me or upset the role-model image I've set. I live a clean, healthy life, and I'm happy about it. I've never done drugs, and I'll never have a reason to do drugs."

"Every city we visit, I get calls from parents with handicapped kids or terminally ill kids whose only wish is to meet Michael Jordan," Bulls media relations director Tim Hallam told Ray Didinger. "The parents say: 'It will only take 10 minutes and it will mean so much.' But they don't realize we have practices and meetings on the road. Maybe Michael has an injury and needs treatment. It's not easy. But I'll ask Michael, and it's incredible what he agrees to do. The last time we were in Washington, D.C., he saw five kids.

"People ask if he ever loses his temper. I can honestly say I've never seen this happen, not once in the seven years I've worked with him. There are times when he will draw the line. If it's a big game, he will say to me: 'Tonight, I'm playing ball.' That means he doesn't want to do interviews or shake hands before the game; he wants to concentrate. But most of the time he's very easy, very accessible."

There was a time just after another game in Washington where Jordan had a rough night in a loss to the Bullets and couldn't fall asleep until almost 2 A.M. Yet he was up at 6:30 and off to George Washington's gym for a special appearance. *USA Today's* Tom Weir accompanied Michael to a workout with kids

One of Jordan's baseball thrills was playing an exhibition game for the White Sox against the crosstown Cubs at Wrigley Field.

involved in the Special Olympics, most of them suffering from Down's syndrome, which often claims the life of its victims before the age of 40. Weir reported that one of them, Freddy Lockett, walked up to Jordan and said: "I've seen you on TV. You ain't that tough." To which Jordan responded: "You and me, Freddy, one-on-one."

"I don't really get sad looking at them," Jordan told Weir. "There's always good with the bad. I'm sad you have situations like this, of course. You know, why can't everybody be like myself? But some of these kids are really competitive. They want to play and they want to learn. I feel I do owe something. With all that I've achieved, this is the least I can do."

Just before he left, Jordan performed a couple of sky dunks that wowed his admirers. Tough little Freddy tried guarding Jordan on one of his moves. "Took you to the hoop," Jordan said with a smile. "But we'll meet up again." As Jordan got up to leave, a little girl named Tania bowed her head and began to cry. Jordan got her attention, told her to look up at him, and gave her a big hug.

Something Michael cherished but never revealed was his special friendship with four young kids in a tough area of Chicago's West Side. Jordan regularly visited the kids after home games, and he eventually demanded to see their report cards to check on their progress in school. It might have remained Michael's secret except that a couple of Bulls fans had their car break down one night across the street from where Jordan held his get-togethers. They saw him talking with the youths.

"It was really a thing with Michael," said his wife, Juanita. "I

Though Jordan's jumper was a little off during his 1994-95 return, he could still jam with the best of them.

think Michael became concerned that his visits were beginning to take over their lives. So, he asked to see their grades to check and see if they were paying attention to their schoolwork."

* * * * * *

"I'm back." With those two words on March 18, 1995, Jordan returned to the Bulls, thus setting the table for the 1995-96 season, in which the Bulls won a record 72 games and Jordan won his eighth scoring title. Why did he come back?

"I love the game," he said. "I had a good opportunity to come back. I tried to stay away as much as I could. I think at the time I walked away from it, I probably needed [the break], mentally more so than anything. But I really, truly missed

Michael was his old self again in 1995-96, leading the league in scoring (30.4 points per game) for a record eighth time.

the game. I missed my friends. I certainly missed my teammates."

And everybody knows that Michael is good for basketball, just as he was for baseball. "Quite frankly, I really felt I wanted to instill some positive things back in the game," he said. "There's a lot of negative things that have been happening, and in terms of me coming back, I do with the notion of the Larry Birds and the Magic Johnsons and the Doctor Js, all those players who paved the road for a lot of young guys. And the young guys are not taking care of their responsibility for maintaining that love for the game. I just think you should respect the game."

DANCING IN THE SHADOWS

With Michael Jordan reclaiming the spotlight, Scottie Pippen finally feels free to do his thing.

Scottie Pippen can only be second best with the Chicago Bulls—no matter how wonderfully he plays. But now he is second to no one else in the league. And that just thrills him.

Being No. 2 never felt so good.

After nine seasons in the NBA, Pippen has found real happiness in his role as the much-acclaimed sidekick to megastar Michael Jordan, the best and most popular player in basketball history. He no longer wonders how much better he could be if he wasn't tailoring his game to Jordan's.

Pippen has been there—during Jordan's brief retirement—done that, and he didn't like what he found, settling that issue in his mind forever, freeing him to fully enjoy his own lofty accomplishments. That freedom makes this incredible championship season feel better than the other three combined.

"I've matured, and I've learned a lot over the years," Pippen said. "The season and a half without Michael taught me some things. I don't feel I ever could be Michael Jordan, or take over his status. I can only be Scottie and hold the ground that I walk on. And I can be very happy with that."

Pippen was as instrumental as anyone in the Bulls' record-setting,

72-victory season. He was second on the team in scoring (19.4 points per game), third in rebounding (6.4), first in assists (5.9), second in steals (1.73), and second in minutes played (36.7).

He staked his claim as the most complete, most versatile player in basketball, plugging in his contributions wherever needed on a particular night. If Jordan was off, Pippen scored more. If Dennis Rodman was

Right and left: *Thrilled to have Michael Jordan by his side again in 1995-96, Pippen was his old self. Smiles were as common as his many dunks, and he was praised for his teamwork and leadership.*

absent, Pippen rebounded more. If Ron Harper needed help defensively, Pippen responded there. What the Bulls needed is what they got from Pippen.

Scottie scored a season-high 40 points in a victory at Indiana. Jordan scored 44 in that same game, making it the first time in 12 years that any pair of NBA teammates both scored 40 or more in a single game. He loved the accomplishment. He loved standing alongside Jordan.

Five times Pippen grabbed a season-high 14 rebounds. He was NBA Player of the Month in December when he averaged 25.5 points, 7.0 rebounds, 6.0 assists, and 2.4 steals. He had a pair of triple-doubles—double figures in scoring, rebounding, and assists. And he reached double-figure scoring in 72 of the

Shaquille O'Neal and Anfernee Hardaway may own richer endorsement deals, but Pippen's the one who's wearing the rings.

77 games he played—a testament to his consistency.

Pippen missed five games during the regular season with tendinitis in his right knee, and he started the other 77. He scored 30 points or more seven times, all of which were victories.

"I think the greatest tribute to Scottie Pippen is that some people consider him the best player in basketball," said Jerry Krause, Bulls vice-president of basketball operations. "And he's playing with the best player who ever played this game. That to me is unbelievable."

While he once chafed—along with many others—under the all-encompassing shadow of Jordan, Pippen has learned to thrive under it, relishing the opportunities it provides. He no longer sees it as a large tree that blocks out the sun,

but a tree that provides some wonderful shade. It is not a blanket that smothers him, but a security blanket.

Without Jordan for almost two years, Pippen played marvelously. During the 1993-94 season, he set career highs in scoring (22.0) and rebounding (8.7). But he almost went nuts, bouncing from one controversy to another, nearly self-

**"I was afraid for him. Everything seemed to build up and boil over."
—Michael Jordan**

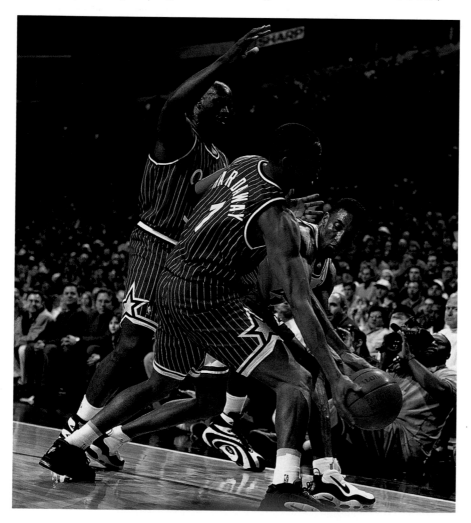

destructing under the strain of carrying the bulk of the load.

Some players blossom when they move out onto their own. Pippen did physically, but he recoiled mentally. Without Jordan to deflect the attention, without Jordan to help carry the load, Pippen felt alone and sometimes lost. The acclaim he had wanted so badly earlier in his career was not like he thought it would be. The bright lights had too much glare. As a celebrity, he struggled.

The problems crested at the end of the 1993-94 season when he did the unthinkable. Pippen was finishing a great season on the court without Jordan, and the Bulls had won 55 games, but the strain was showing at playoff time.

In the second-round series against the rival New York Knicks, Pippen refused to play for the final 1.8 seconds of Game 3—the biggest game of the year because the Bulls trailed 2-0. He was upset that the final shot in a one-point game was being drawn up during a timeout for Toni Kukoc—and not him. So he sat and sulked. Kukoc made the shot and the Bulls won the game, but they lost the series and Pippen lost everyone's respect.

That was just one of several incidents that soiled his reputation after Jordan left. Pippen got into trouble with police for having a gun in his car. He accused Chicago fans of being racist in their support of Kukoc, a white player, over other team members. He blasted management for allowing good friend Horace Grant to leave as a free agent. He blasted his teammates. He feuded with Krause, demanding a trade, demanding a new contract, demanding some satisfaction. He didn't know exactly what he wanted, but he wanted something.

Pippen was almost traded before the 1994-95 season for Seattle's Shawn Kemp, but the deal fell through. Scottie threw a chair onto the court during one game in 1994-95 after a dispute with an official; the league fined and suspended him. Police were called to his home one night because of a domestic dispute. He was involved in a paternity suit. The list grew.

It was a nightmare without Jordan. And the game became more of a burden than a passion, a curse instead of a blessing.

"A lot of negative things happened to him," Jordan said. "But no one had as much sympathy for him as I did. I was afraid for him. Everything seemed to build up and boil over. He had some rough times, but he

THE PIPPEN FILE

Position: Forward/Guard
Height: 6'7" **Weight:** 228
Birth date: September 25, 1965
College: Central Arkansas
NBA Experience: 9 years
Acquired: Traded from Super-Sonics for Olden Polynice and a 2nd-round pick, 6/87

CAREER HIGHLIGHTS

- Four-time NBA champion (1991 through 1993 and 1996)
- Three-time member of All-NBA first team (1993-94 through 1995-96)
- Five-time member of NBA All-Defensive first team (1991-92 through 1995-96)
- Most Valuable Player of 1994 All-Star Game
- Led the NBA in steals in 1994-95
- Olympic gold medalist in 1992

got through them, and he grew from the experience."

When Jordan left baseball and returned to the Bulls in March 1995, Pippen was happier than anyone. He embraced the return, relieved that he could work alongside Michael again. Together, he knew, they could win another championship, and be better than ever. And he would happily play his role.

"I think the year and a half that I wasn't around were helpful to him from a basketball standpoint—to

accept leadership and to know how to apply it in certain situations," Jordan said. "At times now, we can reverse roles, him stepping up and supporting me when I need help. That's a sign of his maturity, and it's helpful for both of us. He and I have been hoping for that for a long time."

When the Bulls traded for enigmatic but always colorful Dennis Rodman last summer, it meant Pippen would move further than ever into the background. And that was just fine with him.

"It doesn't really faze me anymore," Pippen said. "I'm happy to be playing here. I'd be lying if I said I wasn't. I know my value to the team. I've laid it all on the line, and I think everybody knows that now. I've adjusted and done what this team needed. And I've had really a lot of fun this season. It's been a wonderful season all around."

Only during timeouts and blowouts did the Big Three—Michael Jordan, Pippen, and Dennis Rodman—share the pine together.

Left: *Some were surprised when Pippen was named to the Olympic Dream Team in 1992, but he wound up leading the club in assists per game (5.9).* Above: *Scottie has been compared to the great Julius Erving; both could take off from the foul line and dunk spectacularly.*

One regular-season game in particular defined the Jordan/Pippen relationship last season, a hard-fought victory over the Magic in Orlando, the team that had defeated them in the conference semifinals the year before.

Jordan led the Bulls with 27 points, but Pippen led with 13 rebounds. And he provided the defense in the closing minute, smothering Orlando's Anfernee Hardaway on back-to-back possessions. Jordan had guarded Hardaway much of the game, but with the game on the line Pippen took over defensively, covering for his teammate to win the game.

"Confidence-wise, he's 100 percent better," Jordan said. "He really goes out and focuses on the game each night. Last year, he might not have had the positive feelings as far as winning. I think he's more comfortable with what we have. He's more comfortable with himself. He's at peace."

Pippen, maybe the most misunderstood and mysterious of the Bulls' key players, remains a bit of a loner away from the court, too. And that's how he likes it. In his rambling North Shore home, he has built a large saltwater fish tank where he keeps a pair of sharks. He can sit and watch them for hours, watch them gliding through the water, much like he glides down court, ready to strike at any time.

He's a lot like those sharks. They are unusual pets, but he is an unusual person.

"They're an aggressive fish, quiet and attacking. I guess you could say that's like me," he said. "There's probably a lot of truth to that. I kind of have that mentality. Like a shark. I know people think I'm arrogant sometimes, but people don't really know me. I'm human, and I'm happy with who I am and where I am. I've come a long way."

Pippen's rags-to-riches story with the Bulls is one of the more compelling in the league. He is the youngest of 10 children, growing up in a two-bedroom house in Hamburg, Arkansas. His father, a mill worker, suffered a stroke and went on disability before Pippen was in high school. An older brother was crippled in a freak high school gym class accident. Pippen knows how fragile life really is.

He became a skinny, 6'1" point guard at Hamburg High School, but he couldn't attract any college scholarship offers, although he still wanted to keep playing basketball. So he went to Central Arkansas on a work-study grant to become the basketball team manager. He washed other players' clothes, swept the gymnasium, and pushed out the ball racks every day.

He also grew six inches his first year, and he retained some of those point-guard skills he had in high school. By the end of his freshman year, he had earned a basketball scholarship. By the end of his sophomore year, he was the best player on the team. And by the end of his junior year, he was an NBA prospect.

No one realized how good of a prospect he was until after his senior year, when he played in some postseason invitational games. At tiny Central Arkansas, an NAIA school, the competition he faced was weak, which made evaluating him difficult. Those long arms and those long, lean strides were obvious, but no one knew how tough he was.

In a prearranged gamble, the Bulls had Seattle select him fifth in the 1987 draft, then sent the rights to Olden Polynice (drafted eighth) and a draft pick to Seattle in exchange. Seattle still regrets that trade. The Bulls have four championships to show for it. Without Pippen, none would have come to Chicago.

"I had a lot to learn, a lot to get used to when I first came into the league," Pippen said. "It wasn't always easy, but I always tried to learn something from each experience. Let's just say the transition was a big one for me."

For Pippen, coming to the NBA from Central Arkansas was like coming from high school. He had never been to an NBA game before his debut. Central Arkansas had never traveled by plane. Pippen arrived both wide-eyed and suspicious.

"I think Scottie really benefited from having Michael around at the start of his career," said Doug Collins, coach of the Bulls during Pippen's rookie season. "He learned

> **"They're an aggressive fish, quiet and attacking. I guess you could say that's like me. . . . I kind of have that mentality. Like a shark."**
> —Scottie Pippen

Pippen and Michael Jordan celebrate the Bulls' 1992 NBA Finals triumph over Portland. It was the first time they won the title at home.

Left: *Forced to do it all in 1994-95, Pippen led the Bulls in points, rebounds, assists, and steals. Mentally, though, he couldn't handle the load.* Right: *Scottie displays his 1992-93 Fleer Ultra basketball card.*

what the game was all about from the best. No one let him cut corners, and he was in a competitive situation in practice every day. I don't want to say he was the baby of the family, but when he got to Chicago, he was still a very young man who was having his eyes opened for the first time."

Pippen still returns every summer to Arkansas and stays with family and friends. He runs a basketball camp in Conway, near the university he attended. Shortly after signing his current contract, he built his mother a new house, then built several homes for several other relatives all in the same area, creating his own neighborhood.

And that's where he likes to go in the summer.

"I just like to be around family," Pippen said. "And friends. If you're one of my friends, you're not even going to know I'm an NBA player. I don't ever try to be more than anyone else because I'm not. I've always thought that one injury could wipe all of this away. I'm able to run and jump and do all the things I can do. I'm blessed. We're all

blessed in the NBA, and we can't lose sight of how lucky we are."

In Pippen's first season with the Bulls, he sustained a back injury that eventually would require surgery, but doctors didn't diagnose the problem for almost a year. He played in pain, but he was quietly accused of being soft and lacking

the drive to really perform. It was a frustrating time for him.

It was always Jordan who pushed him to excel, sometimes to the point of tears, and he wondered often if he would be better off somewhere else.

"In the early years, he wanted to be like Michael," said former team-

PIPPEN'S NBA REGULAR-SEASON STATISTICS

| | | G | MIN | FGs | | 3-PT FGs | | FTs | | Rebounds | | AST | STL | BLK | PTS | PPG |
				FG	PCT	FG	PCT	FT	PCT	OFF	TOT					
1987-88	CHI	79	1650	261	.463	4	.174	99	.576	115	298	169	91	52	625	7.9
1988-89	CHI	73	2413	413	.476	21	.273	201	.668	138	445	256	139	61	1048	14.4
1989-90	CHI	82	3148	562	.489	28	.250	199	.675	150	547	444	211	101	1351	16.5
1990-91	CHI	82	3014	600	.520	21	.309	240	.706	163	595	511	193	93	1461	17.8
1991-92	CHI	82	3164	687	.506	16	.200	330	.760	185	630	572	155	93	1720	21.0
1992-93	CHI	81	3123	628	.473	22	.237	232	.663	203	621	507	173	73	1510	18.6
1993-94	CHI	72	2759	627	.491	63	.320	270	.660	173	629	403	211	58	1587	22.0
1994-95	CHI	79	3014	634	.480	109	.345	315	.716	175	639	409	232	89	1692	21.4
1995-96	CHI	77	2825	563	.463	150	.374	220	.679	152	496	452	133	57	1496	19.4
Totals		707	25110	4975	.486	434	.317	2106	.687	1454	4900	3723	1538	677	12490	17.7

mate Horace Grant. "But after awhile, when Michael didn't treat him how he liked, that would bother him. But something always brought him back to Michael, looking for acceptance."

Pippen has been lucky enough, and good enough, to compile an impressive list of accomplishments in his career, even though he wondered if that career would ever get off the ground. Pippen became an All-Star for the first time in 1990,

> **"In the early years, he wanted to be like Michael. But after awhile, when Michael didn't treat him how he liked, that would bother him. But something always brought him back to Michael, looking for acceptance."**
> **—Horace Grant**

but that also was the season he suffered a migraine headache in the playoffs and was blamed for the Bulls' series loss to Detroit.

Pippen, through the ups and downs, remained fiercely proud, a trait he developed in his early years. It intensified watching Jordan. He still doesn't admit any fault in his

Used by the Bulls as a "point forward," Pippen will occasionally uncork a Magic-like pass. During the 1990s, no other forward has tallied as many assists as Pip.

Pippen jams over Milwaukee's Sherman Douglas. Scottie was Player of the Month in December 1995, averaging 25.5 points, 7.0 rebounds, and 6.0 assists.

sit-down protest against the Knicks, nor has he apologized for all the name-calling with Krause.

He has returned to that All-Star Game every year since, except one. He was the MVP of the All-Star Game in 1994. He played on the 1992 Olympic Dream Team in Barcelona, and he'll play again this summer on Dream Team III, the next Olympic team, in Atlanta.

Scottie has been selected to the NBA's All-Defensive first team five times. He was a key performer on the three previous NBA championship teams (1991, '92, and '93). But none of that felt as good as this

last one, back playing alongside Jordan for another championship ring.

For most of two seasons, the Bulls were Pippen's team. Now with the furor over Rodman and Jordan, Pippen is deeper in the shadows than he has been in years. Reporters and fans often rush past in their haste to get closer to the other two. Pippen, now 30, just smiles. He knows where he stands, and he is comfortable with that stance.

There were no more demands for a new contract this past season, no more battles with management, no more sit-downs because he didn't get the ball.

"Every day he brought a new element to our team, not only playing well but showing his leadership on the court," Chicago coach Phil Jackson said. "He's the guy who takes us and leads us offensively and de-

fensively. He's been extremely active. Without him, none of this would have been possible. He just may be the most complete player in the game."

Jordan won the league MVP Award by a landslide this past season, but even he said he thought Pippen might have been the MVP of the Bulls in their record-setting season. He likes to think of himself and Pippen as partners, not No. 1 and No. 2, which will always be the way they are perceived.

"I know some things I've said or things I've done haven't always been understood," Pippen said. "But if it comes down to speaking your feelings or doing what you have to do, you're cheating yourself if you don't voice your opinion. I've done that, and I have no regrets. It's all worked out just fine."

I DID IT MY WAY

Dennis Rodman dyed his hair, revved his bike, and drove full throttle to the NBA championship.

When Dennis Rodman arrived in Chicago last summer, there was nothing left for him to pierce, dye, or tattoo. So he did the next most enjoyable thing he could imagine.

He helped lead the Chicago Bulls to a record-setting season and another NBA title. And he did it on his terms, in his own unique style.

He did it on the court, winning a fifth consecutive rebounding title, providing the interior defense the Bulls previously lacked, and creating a spark of confidence that spread through every member of the team.

He did it with his own eccentricity, deflecting the pressure and the spotlight that previously had fallen squarely on the shoulders of superstars Michael Jordan and Scottie Pippen.

He did it by making them laugh. And he did it by making them cry. But he always did it by making them better, playing with the boundless energy of a rookie coupled with the championship knowhow of a veteran.

"I just did what I do best," Rodman said late in the season. "This is what I've been doing for the last eight or nine years. For the last two or three years, though, everybody was knocking Dennis Rodman

Anxious to drum up publicity for his new book, Bad as I Wanna Be, ***Rodman showed up at a book-signing in this outrageous get-up.***

about all the things he had done that were wrong. But nobody ever liked to praise Dennis Rodman for all the good things he did. I've always been on winning teams, and I've always been productive. Hopefully, I've been entertaining, too."

From the multicolored hair to the multiholed body, from the bizarre behavior to the kinky things he revealed in his recent book, Rodman gave what already was the league's

most popular team an aura that went well beyond sports. People were attracted by his rebel image, others repulsed by his vulgarity as he overstepped the bounds of good taste. But both sides were captivated by his peculiarity. They were fascinated by him like they would be fascinated by a car wreck on the highway, impossible to drive past without slowing for a glance.

It's hard to imagine anyone stealing the spotlight from a megastar like Jordan—the greatest player in basketball history—but it happened with Rodman, much to Jordan's delight. Jordan remained the centerpiece of the Bulls, but Rodman became such a curiosity that he allowed Jordan to slip in and out of the locker room and other settings without always being mobbed by reporters or fans. They were too busy with Rodman.

"I love having Dennis around," Jordan said as he slipped past the normal media horde crowded around Rodman. "It's different. It's interesting and it's fun."

If not for his 14.9 rebounds per game, which provided take-out

In 1995-96, Rodman joined Moses Malone as the only players in NBA history to lead the league in rebounding five years in a row.

service for Jordan and Pippen's offense, Rodman's unique persona might have been his greatest contribution to the magnificent season.

"Dennis has brought more enthusiasm to this team with his play than we ever expected," said Jerry Krause, Bulls vice-president of basketball operations, who ultimately made the decision to trade for Rodman last summer. "He was electric every night, and that rubbed off on his teammates."

Rodman was electric, all right. He played like he was plugged into a body battery that kept him charged

> **"I'm not just glitter and hype. I think that fans appreciated that. This is a blue-collar town, and they appreciate hard work."**
> **—Dennis Rodman**

full-time. Even at age 34, he was still a quick and relentless jumper with an uncanny knack for gauging where the rebounds would be.

He still loped up and down the court like a frisky colt, doing his endless tip drills that eventually resulted in rebounds, keeping the ball alive until he could grab it. He would sprint up-court to follow fastbreaks, then punch the air with the ferocity of a prizefighter when the Bulls scored.

People forget that beyond that punk-rock body is a tireless worker who already had two championship

With the two-time champion Pistons, Rodman was a coach's dream who provided rebounding, defense, and energy off the bench.

After battling depression in Detroit, Dennis was traded to San Antonio, dyed his hair, and became the league's No. 1 rebel.

rings from his years with the Detroit Pistons during their Bad Boy days.

"I went out there and busted my butt every night," Rodman said. "I didn't take nights off. I was brought in to do the dirty work, and I did it. I'm not just glitter and hype. I think the fans appreciated that. This is a blue-collar town, and they appreciate hard work."

What they also loved was his showmanship. After games, he gave away his Bulls jersey, causing huge commotions at home and on the road as fans jockeyed for position to catch his attention as he left the court.

At one stop, there were young boys wearing Rodman T-shirts, women holding up banners that offered to trade shirts, kids in wheelchairs, middle-aged men clamoring like children. And there was Rodman, stripping to his waist, showing off the sculpted body and his tattooed arms, back, and navel, tossing the jersey into the stands.

Rodman, though, became a walking contradiction, flirting with the fine line between entertainment and going mad.

His head-butt of an official late in the season cost him a six-game suspension, the wrath of Jordan, and extra-close scrutiny from game and league officials every night through the remainder of the season. He was ejected three times during the campaign and received 28 technical fouls. Some of them were showstoppers, and some of them were just plain foolish.

"I made a mistake, a big one (with the head-butt)," Rodman admitted. "I lost my temper and did something I shouldn't have done, because it hurt the team and disappointed a lot of fans. But when I played, nobody can say that I didn't give 110 percent. I played for the

team, and I played for the fans. I'm no fool. I am happy in Chicago, and I wanted people to know that I could still help teams win championships."

It wasn't exactly entertainment value the Bulls had in mind when they traded Will Perdue to San Antonio for Rodman last summer. Krause and the rest of the staff spent a month analyzing their playoff failure the previous season. They knew what was lacking.

Horace Grant, the dirty-work power forward for the Bulls' three championship teams (1991, '92, and '93) left for Orlando in 1994, making the Magic a title contender and leaving a huge hole in Chicago. It was Orlando that defeated the Bulls in last year's playoffs, and Grant played a major role from both sides.

"What happens in this league is you point to the top team, see what

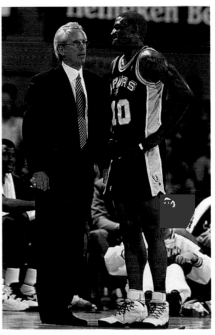

San Antonio coach Bob Hill couldn't wait to dump Rodman, whose rule-breaking shenanigans sabotaged the Spurs in the playoffs.

their strength is, and make adjustments," said Bulls guard Steve Kerr. "Adding Dennis was obviously geared toward Orlando. He turned out to be our missing ingredient, just like many of us felt he would. He helped us all get a lot of extra shots."

Rodman had won his fourth consecutive rebounding title the previous season in San Antonio, but his outrageousness on and off the court frustrated the Spurs. Unable to deal with his temperament, they traded him to one of the few teams with a coach, Phil Jackson, who saw Rodman as a challenge instead of a problem.

"I like Dennis," Jackson said. "He has his moments when he'll test you, and I don't always understand him, but I understand how he works. I think he's found a home in Chicago with the Bulls."

Before they made the trade, the Bulls spent several days discussing his merits, meeting with Dennis and trying to figure him out. Krause and Jackson consulted with Jordan and Pippen, who both encouraged his

THE RODMAN FILE

Position: Forward
Height: 6'8" **Weight:** 220
Birth date: May 13, 1961
NBA Experience: 10 years
College: S.E. Oklahoma St.
Acquired: Traded by Spurs for Will Perdue, 10/95

CAREER HIGHLIGHTS

◎ Three-time NBA champion (1989, 1990, and 1996)

◎ Five-time NBA rebounding champion (1991-92 through 1995-96)

◎ Two-time NBA Defensive Player of the Year (1989-90 and 1990-91)

◎ Seven-time member of NBA All-Defensive first team (1988-89 through 1992-93, 1994-95, and 1995-96)

◎ Led NBA in field-goal percentage in 1988-89

adding different players instead, but no one of Rodman's ability.

When the Bulls made the trade, there was the expected skepticism, from media, from fans, and even from his own new teammates. Rodman had submarined the championship hopes of the Spurs the

didn't mean it would affect our playing together."

Rodman was uncharacteristically subdued early in training camp, aware that this might be his final chance to win another title. He was in the final year of his contract, and he understood his future would rest on this season. He was strangely low-key in preseason, until he was asked to address a luncheon of Bulls fans and sponsors. It was there he issued his first challenge to his teammates.

"People on this team are going to have to have the same attitude that I do, guys like Luc Longley and other guys who don't have the fire," Rodman said then. "I don't give a damn if Luc turns around and punches me in the face. If that is what it is going to take to get him going, go right ahead. Hit me."

Those words proved prophetic. Early in the regular season, the normally mild-mannered Longley went aggressively after a rebound, swing-

> ❝I don't give a damn if Luc turns around and punches me in the face. If that is what it is going to take to get him going, go right ahead. Hit me.❞
> —Dennis Rodman

addition. At one meeting at Krause's home, Jackson arrived on his motorcycle, much to Rodman's delight. The two understood each other well.

Although Jordan and Pippen—usually businesslike—didn't always appreciate Rodman's bizarre behavior, they encouraged his arrival because they knew it would help win another championship. And Jordan was confident he was strong enough to keep Rodman focused on the court. The Bulls considered

previous season, picking fights with San Antonio coach Bob Hill, and many teams wouldn't touch him. But he arrived in Chicago on his best behavior, won the respect of his new teammates, and made a difference from the start.

"I'll never forget what he did to me when he was playing for Detroit," said Pippen, referring to the push in the back at the end of one fastbreak that sent Pippen face first into the basket stanchion. "But that

Thanks to Rodman, the Bulls out-rebounded foes by 541 in 1995-96—tops in the league and a 461-board improvement over 1994-95.

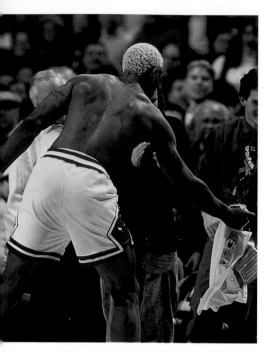

When Rodman took off his jersey after games, fans clamored like concertgoers for the garment. Dennis usually gave it to a kid.

I think people see I am not a fake, a glitter-type guy. I am a guy who puts his heart and soul on the floor. I am a guy who likes to go out and, if necessary, break an arm, get his nose busted to win a basketball game."

It was also early when Rodman mocked Alonzo Mourning for turning down a $10 million-per-year contract offer from the Charlotte Hornets and forcing his trade to Miami. Mourning, he said, was an example of how young players look at professional basketball.

"They don't care about the game of basketball," Rodman said. "Like Alonzo Mourning saying no to $10 million a year. You tell me: Is he worried about the game of basketball or about the money?"

It didn't take long for the Bulls to realize they had found a replacement for Grant, probably even improved upon him with Rodman. Yes, Dennis was a little skewed, but he wasn't a round peg trying to fit into a square hole, like some suspected.

"I'm happy with the Bulls, I always have been," Rodman said. "And that's because they let me be me. They don't give a darn about what you do, as long as you do what you have to do. In San Antonio, they were always worried about what I was doing off the court, afraid that I might embarrass them."

Though Grant's strengths were defense and rebounding, Rodman did them both even better. His exceptionally long arms and quick feet made him an ideal defender to trap ball-handlers. He was the Defensive Player of the Year in 1990 and '91 with Detroit, and he has made the NBA's All-Defensive first team seven times.

> **"They don't care about the game of basketball. Like Alonzo Mourning saying no to $10 million a year. You tell me: Is he worried about the game of basketball or about money?"**
> **—Dennis Rodman**

He relished the challenge of taking on the opposing team's best offensive player regardless of position. He didn't back down from centers, yet he was agile enough to cover forwards when the situation demanded.

ing his elbows wildly after finally corralling it. One of the elbows caught Rodman in the jaw, knocking him back a few steps. Rodman grabbed his chin, shook his head a few times, then whacked Longley on the behind. "That's what I'm talking about, Luc," he told him.

"I am a throwback, and a lot of people in Chicago are throwbacks," Rodman said. "They work their butts off just to get a little bit and make themselves happy and proud.

RODMAN'S NBA REGULAR-SEASON STATISTICS

		G	MIN	FGs FG	FGs PCT	3-PT FGs FG	3-PT FGs PCT	FTs FT	FTs PCT	Rebounds OFF	Rebounds TOT	AST	STL	BLK	PTS	PPG
1986-87	DET	77	1155	213	.545	0	.000	74	.587	163	332	56	38	48	500	6.5
1987-88	DET	82	2147	398	.561	5	.294	152	.535	318	715	110	75	45	953	11.6
1988-89	DET	82	2208	316	.595	6	.231	97	.626	327	772	99	55	76	735	9.0
1989-90	DET	82	2377	288	.581	1	.111	142	.654	336	792	72	52	60	719	8.8
1990-91	DET	82	2747	276	.493	6	.200	111	.631	361	1026	85	65	55	669	8.2
1991-92	DET	82	3301	342	.539	32	.317	84	.600	523	1530	191	68	70	800	9.8
1992-93	DET	62	2410	183	.427	15	.205	87	.534	367	1132	102	48	45	468	7.5
1993-94	SA	79	2989	156	.534	5	.208	53	.520	453	1367	184	52	32	370	4.7
1994-95	SA	49	1568	137	.571	0	.000	75	.676	274	823	97	31	23	349	7.1
1995-96	CHI	64	2088	146	.480	3	.111	56	.528	356	952	160	36	27	351	5.5
Totals		741	22990	2455	.535	73	.235	931	.589	3478	9441	1156	520	481	5914	8.0

Rodman seemingly poses for the camera after a rebound. While teammates avoided the limelight, Rodman actively sought it.

"Horace was a good defender, but Dennis has the reputation for really playing defense," Pippen said. "Dennis can guard anybody, smaller guys or bigger guys. He came in here and did exactly what we expected him to do."

It was at the offensive end of the floor that the difference between Grant and Rodman went from subtle to glaring. Grant liked to be considered part of the attack. He often grew frustrated that Jordan and Pippen took most of the shots, leaving few for him or anyone else. Rodman doesn't care if he ever shoots.

"With Dennis, we gained the best offensive rebounder this game has seen in a long time," Jackson said. "I can't remember another one. You gain more shots at the basket with him. And that becomes so important in a tight game."

Rodman became the provider for second shots, happy to toss out his offensive rebounds to the 3-point shooters. He finished with 5.6 offensive boards per game, easily the most in the league. He got the fans as excited about his offensive rebounding as some scorers do with 3-point shots or dunks.

"Horace was more offensive-minded, but Dennis is more fun, because you are always waiting on something to happen," said Pippen, who still is one of Grant's closest friends. "You wait for him to get that offensive rebound and get the crowd going. He does the little things that get the momentum and the energy of a game going."

Grant was diligent, but rarely demonstrative in doing the job for the Bulls. Rodman, conversely, was like a blowtorch, lighting a fire under the Bulls at any time.

"Horace was tough, but not as nasty and didn't have that defiance that Dennis shows," said assistant

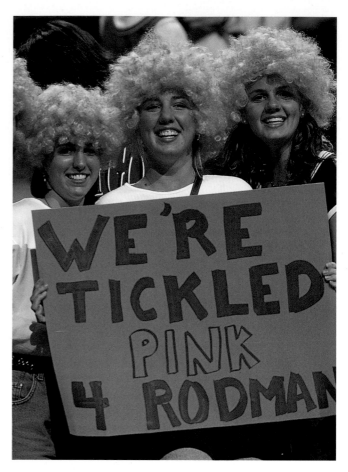

Left: *Times have surely changed since the 1991 playoffs, when Chicagoans hated Rodman for cheap-shotting Scottie Pippen.* **Right:** *Every night was Halloween at the United Center, as fans outdid each other with their Rodman costumes.*

coach John Paxson, who was a player on the three earlier championship teams. "Horace would get into a little bit of a funk when his offensive game wasn't going, and you had to urge him to contribute in other areas."

Rodman needed no encouraging to play hard, just some reminders to make sure his contributions were toward winning first and entertainment second. His style was a curiosity to teammates, but it often frustrated opponents.

He flustered Milwaukee's Glenn Robinson to the point where Robinson had to leave a game after receiving a technical foul for cursing and finger pointing at Rodman.

"I'm pretty sure [Robinson] is one of the guys in the league who hates me," Rodman said. "If he wants to lash out because he makes $6 million or $7 million and hasn't done anything in this league, that's great. He can mouth off all he wants, but I've proven myself. I've dedicated myself to work hard and being happy."

It was not a perfect season, but it never is with Rodman. He missed 12 games early with a strained left calf. He was suspended for six after the head butt. He played as a reserve for seven games, leaving his starting role to Toni Kukoc.

What he did was remind people of a younger Rodman in his glory years, the player who chased every rebound, dived after loose balls, defended relentlessly while grabbing, holding, and pushing to get the job done.

That's when he wasn't so popular, when he wasn't so antiestablish-

ment, when he wasn't so peculiar.

Rodman started his career in Detroit, a little-known second-round pick from Southeastern Oklahoma State. He played there after a year in junior college and another year sweeping floors as a janitor, a young man going nowhere fast. But college basketball may have saved him, and the Pistons nurtured him.

Detroit coach Chuck Daly became the father figure he never had, and Rodman began to flourish. However, when the team broke apart following its back-to-back championships, Rodman felt like he was losing a family. Daly left, Rodman's marriage broke up, and he drifted. He was found one night alone in the parking lot at the Palace of Auburn Hills, in his truck with a gun in his lap.

When things got uncomfortable for both sides, the Pistons traded him to San Antonio, where he only got weirder when they tried to make him conform. That's when the hair started to change colors. When he was dealt to Chicago, the colors exploded.

Rodman's popularity grew to the point that his picture was painted on the side of a building near downtown Chicago, right next to the one of Jordan. Rodman's picture was designed so that the hair color could be changed regularly.

The mural was visible from the expressway, which immediately

> **❝If [Glenn Robinson] wants to lash out because he makes $6 million or $7 million and hasn't done anything in this league, that's great. He can mouth off all he wants, but I've proven myself.❞**
> **—Dennis Rodman**

caused serious traffic problems as motorists slowed down to look, much like they would at an accident on the side of the road. It caused such a furor that the Department of Transportation ordered it to be taken down.

"Whoever thought I'd be as popular as I am today?" Rodman asked. "I surely never did. But now all of a sudden, people have opened up and realized, that's just Dennis."

Referees whistled Rodman for 28 technical fouls in 1995-96, putting him just one behind league leader Charles Barkley. Dennis was ejected three times.

THE SUPPORTING CAST

Michael, Scottie, and Dennis would like to thank the cast and crew for making it all possible.

If you appeared in a movie with Tom Hanks, Sharon Stone, and Harrison Ford, you'd realize quickly that your screen time would be limited. Such was the case with the Bulls in 1995-96, as the names of Michael Jordan, Scottie Pippen, and Dennis Rodman filled up nearly every inch of the marquee. The other 12 guys who appeared on Chicago's roster had to settle for supporting roles, bit parts, and—in the case of Jack Haley—a cameo (one game).

Coach Phil Jackson, who directed this award-winning show, did a masterful job of sublimating egos.

Above: The Bulls earned raves for their focus and intensity. Right: Center Luc Longley flips in two.

Spike Lee and Gene Siskel know a good cast when they see one.

Two of his players had once been major stars: Ron Harper, a former 20-a-game scorer, was nicknamed "Hollywood," and Toni Kukoc was once Europe's top box office attraction. But for the good of the big picture, Harper accepted the humble role of defensive stopper, while Kukoc went on to capture the Sixth Man Award, the NBA's version of Best Supporting Actor.

Other Bulls had small but clearly defined roles: Steve Kerr and Jud Buechler offered perimeter shooting, Luc Longley clogged the lane defensively, Randy Brown hounded water bug point guards, and Bill Wennington and James Edwards provided offense from the center position. Though they played little, John Salley and Haley lifted everybody's spirits with their humor and good cheer.

While Jordan, Pippen, and Rodman provided most of the drama, they wouldn't have won the big prize if it weren't for the diligent work and humble attitudes of the supporting cast. It's no wonder that Gene Siskel sat courtside at Bulls home games, giving the entire Bulls team two enthusiastic thumbs up.

PHIL JACKSON

His record as a coach tops everybody else's, yet he is still often taken for granted amidst the superstars and lively personalities on his team. That's fine by him; in fact, it's just the way he wants it.

Phil Jackson stood calmly by in coat and tie during the 1995-96 season as Michael, Scottie, Dennis, and the rest trotted out each day for work. And as the victories piled up, his expression rarely changed. Through a 72-10 regular season and all the way to Chicago's fourth world championship in his seven years at the helm, Jackson remained so reserved that more than a few folks believed the Bulls could have managed themselves to a title.

Even while his players were whooping it up in the final seconds of their record-breaking 70th win, he was content sitting off to the side, hands in his lap. Looking more like a Psych professor than a basketball coach with his graying beard and horn-rimmed glasses, he had no interest in seeking camera time or credit.

Not that he didn't have good reason. Great players may make average coaches look great, but in the complicated world of the modern multimillion-dollar athlete, there are more challenges than ever that come with managing top talent. Jackson has survived a three-year span during which he had to cope with: Michael Jordan's sudden retirement and reemergence, the shock waves throughout the squad that accompanied both moves, bizarre behavior by Scottie Pippen in the 1994 playoffs (when, angered that a play wasn't called for him, he removed himself from a game with 1.8 seconds left), and—most recently—the ever-entertaining saga of Dennis Rodman. That Jackson

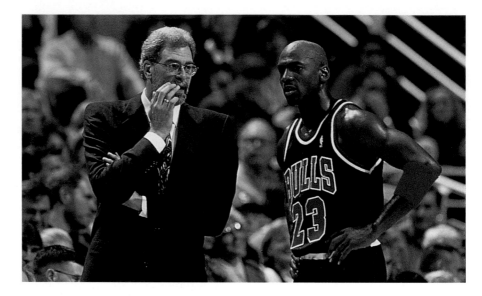

stayed sane during the 1995-96 season was impressive enough; keeping everyone smiling while winning 72 games and another title without a true point guard or first-rate center was nothing short of genius.

"He's so confident, he doesn't have to rant and rave," longtime Bulls guard (and now assistant coach) John Paxson said of Jackson, a 50-year-old Clark Kent-like figure who was named 1995-96 NBA Coach of the Year. "He's even keeled, and it's rubbed off," said Paxson. "It's why we play with the poise we do."

The 1995-96 Bulls kept this poise even after a 41-3 start all but settled the Eastern Conference playoff race, further testament that their coach had the Midas touch. Assistants ranging from the young (Paxson and Jim Cleamons) to the middle-aged (Jimmy Rodgers, who at 53 already has 30-odd years of coaching on his resume) to the ancient (74-year-old Tex Winter, who finished his 11th season with the Bulls and 49th coaching at the collegiate or professional level) all play a role, for there appears to be no generation gaps on this team.

"Phil has a calming influence on everybody," said Michael Jordan. "That's why he's the best."

Jackson's handling of the greatest player in NBA history is perhaps his most impressive accomplishment. When Jackson took over in 1989, Jordan was already the league's biggest talent, but he was still considered a one-man gang. By expanding the skills and responsibilities of the players around MJ, Jackson gave opponents more to worry about and his own team more confidence. The result was a run of three straight championships, then a couple near-misses. Even when Jordan was taking aim at outfield fences instead of hoops during the 1993-94 season, Jackson still coaxed 55 victories out of the team before falling to the New York Knicks in a hard-fought Eastern finals series. "Phil has a calming influence on everybody," Jordan said. "That's why he's the best."

A student of both philosophy and the Grateful Dead while starring at center for the University of North Dakota, Jackson and his wide, 6'8" body fit right in among the diverse personalities that made up the Knicks of the early 1970s—and he was a key role-player on New York's 1972-73 championship club that epitomized team harmony. After 13 workmanlike NBA seasons (6.7 points per game) and short flings as a health club manager and TV color commentator, Jackson spent five seasons as a coach in the no-frills CBA. Turned down by Bulls GM Jerry Krause following his first interview for an assistant-coaching slot with Chicago in the mid-1980s (Krause supposedly objected to his stubble and feathered Panama hat), Phil eventually lost the hat, shaved, and was on Doug Collins's staff by 1987.

From there, things moved quickly. When Collins was ejected from a game with the Bulls down by 14 on December 17, 1988, Jackson took over, immediately implemented a new defensive approach, and told the team to "just go out and play." Chicago won, the players loved Phil's style, and after a playoff loss to Detroit the following spring Collins was fired and Jackson made head coach. Once in charge for good, he further emphasized the strong defense and team-oriented style he had seen succeed firsthand with the Knicks.

Jackson was even able to get His Airness to cooperate with an offense in which the ball came to him a little less often, and within two years the Bulls were champs and Michael was en route to three straight NBA Finals MVP Awards. After title No. 4, the guy who helped make it all happen couldn't be happier—even if nobody outside the locker room seems to notice.

Jackson passed Pat Riley to notch the all-time best regular-season winning percentage at .721.

7 TONI KUKOC

For a man from another country, Toni Kukoc has no trouble getting his point across.

During most of his first two years living in America and playing for the Bulls, the 6'10" Croatian struggled with English yet communicated quite clearly his displeasure over not being allowed to start on a regular basis. He craved the extra attention he knew would come with such a role, and he wanted to be "a Michael or a Scottie" as he had been in Europe.

But this was the NBA, he was told, a league where entire games were played at a frenetic pace and defense was more than just an afterthought. No matter how he felt about it, the three-time European Player of the Year would have to hone his skills and wait his turn.

Kukoc's first shot at a starting spot came late in the 1994-95 season, and Toni responded nicely with a 14.9 average in the role over Chicago's final 37 games. Starting all 10 playoff contests, he kept up his steady scoring while notching nearly seven rebounds and six assists a game. He had proven up to the task, but when the team sent Will Perdue to San Antonio for Dennis Rodman in the off-season, there was really no question what the move meant. Rodman would go into Chicago's starting five, and Kukoc would go back to the bench.

Through the first 60 games, that's where he stayed. Rodman was leading the league in rebounding, Jordan and Pippen were doing their thing, and the Bulls were a fantastic 54-6. Toni was averaging 11.4 points, 3.8 rebounds, and 3.2 assists in just over 23 minutes per game. But then Pippen was forced to the sidelines with tendinitis in his right knee on March 13, and Kukoc was inserted into Scottie's starting slot.

Suddenly, Toni found himself in the middle of the craziness, as Chicago raced down the stretch drive in its attempt to set a league record for victories.

There was concern Chicago would lose a step without the man many considered the NBA's second-best player, but Kukoc silenced it. He had a season-high 10 assists on March 15 vs. Denver, and when Scottie came back and Rodman drew a six-game suspension for head-butting a referee in the same week, Toni stayed in the starting

Above: *Kukoc won the 1995-96 NBA Sixth Man Award, receiving 45 of 113 possible votes. Right: In the 20 games he started, Toni averaged 17.7 points per game.*

lineup—where he remained even after The Worm came back. The Bulls went 18-3 over the period to get their win record, and Kukoc was drawing praises as one of the league's most multitalented big men with great court vision and an outstanding outside touch.

The numbers were terrific: In the 20 games he started, Kukoc averaged 17.7 points, 4.5 rebounds, and 4.4 assists. He had 24 points on 10-of-12 shooting (including 4-of-4 from the 3-point line) against Atlanta March 28. A week later, Kukoc torched the Heat for a career-high 34—including 18 points in the third quarter alone. "Starting is agreeing with me," he said after the latter contest. But when asked if he thought he was going to be made a regular starter, he answered simply: "No." He was enjoying his fame, but he knew better than to think it would last.

His clutch performances drew praise from all. After Kukoc helped spark a win over Orlando with five 3-pointers and 20 points, Anfernee Hardaway of the Magic echoed the thoughts of many throughout the league. "Toni really surprised me," he said. "He really earned my respect. I didn't think Toni Kukoc could do it every game, and he's doing it now."

Jordan admitted his teammate had "taken a lot of the pressure away from myself and Scottie." And when the Bulls notched their record-clinching win at Milwaukee April 16, Kukoc ran around with a huge grin and used his improving English to tell one writer, "The last few minutes were very exciting, and now we are history." Four weeks later, Toni captured the NBA's Sixth Man Award.

Kukoc says he still misses his family back in Croatia, and he hasn't ruled out returning to play in Europe when his Bulls contract expires in five years. For now, however, he's happy to stay put. His defense, conditioning, and on-court smarts have all improved drastically, and his only regret about coming to play in the States is that he waited until he was 25 to do so. He has accepted the challenge and thrived in it—and now he has a championship ring to show for his efforts.

13 LUC LONGLEY

Famous for being the first Australian to play in the NBA, Luc Longley did little else to distinguish himself during his initial four pro seasons. A major disappointment with the woeful Minnesota Timberwolves (who had made him the seventh pick in the 1991 draft), the 7'2" Aussie came to the Bulls midway through the 1993-94 season and provided capable backup at center and forward for the Eastern Conference runners-up.

Bigger things were expected of him after star forward Horace Grant's departure for Orlando the following year, but Luc missed much of the first two months in 1994-95 with a stress fracture in his left leg and failed to win a starting spot upon his return. His dedication to the game was questioned, and when the Bulls came up against Orlando in the playoffs, it was Longley who missed an easy bucket in the closing moments of the last game. It began to appear that Luc's name would eventually be little more than a trivia question in his homeland.

Then opportunity knocked. The Will Perdue-Dennis Rodman trade

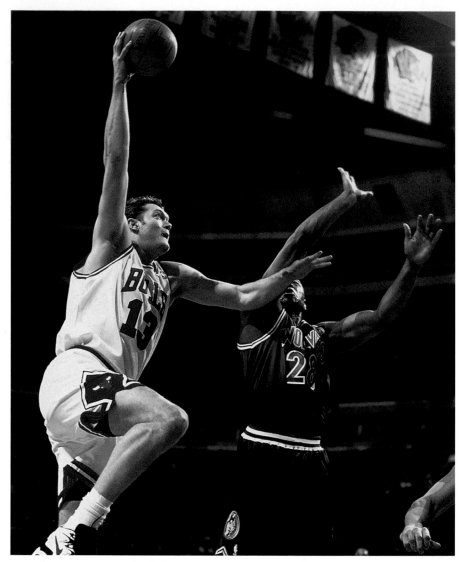

Longley set a career high last season with 9.1 points per game.

Once considered a softy, Luc toughened up in 1995-96.

gave the Bulls the league's best rebounder but left them without a big body to take Perdue's spot in the paint. Longley was the logical choice, and while he didn't burst forth with an All-Star season, he did make significant progress toward fulfilling his potential. After averaging 5.9 points and 4.7 rebounds over his first four years, the former honorable-mention All-American from the University of New Mexico upped the numbers to 9.1 and 5.1 while starting all 62 games he

played. He missed 19 contests with knee problems but still managed to score in double figures 28 times, with a high of 21 against Seattle November 26. He provided stronger defensive pressure in the middle than ever before, and he was the biggest cog in Chicago's center-rotation known as the "three-headed monster."

Though not a superstar, Longley can now be assured his name will be remembered on at least two continents.

9 RON HARPER

It has often been said by ardent NBA followers that a true superstar improves the play of those around him. This being the case, Ron Harper amazed more than a few people when he went from being a star in his own right to a flop almost overnight after teaming up with a couple fellows named Jordan and Pippen. Harper had averaged 18 or more points in seven of his eight seasons in the league when he came to Chicago in 1994-95, but the 6'6" guard never seemed comfortable in the Bulls' triangle offense and saw his output plummet from 20.1 to 6.9 points per game in one year.

Harper was actually expected to replace Jordan when he first joined the Bulls with a five-year, $19-million contract. But when Michael suddenly came back, Harper lost his starting role. He had been struggling long before MJ's return, and with Jordan at full strength for 1995-96, not much was expected from Harper. Chalking up

Harper (105 steals) contributed to the Bulls' smothering team defense.

the previous year to transition and poor conditioning, Ron came back in great shape ready to accept whatever role offered him.

Winning back his starting spot, Harper raised his average only slightly (to 7.4 points per game), but he saw his shooting percentage leap from 43 to 47 percent and his rebounding, assists, and steals totals all go up. His hustle also made him one of the most popular players on the squad. "We've got enough scorers on this team, and Ron realizes there are other ways to take advantage of his skills," assistant coach Jim Cleamons explained. "His defense on shooting guards has been outstanding."

Once a local boy who made good as the all-time leading scorer at Miami of Ohio and as NBA Rookie of the Year runner-up with the Cavaliers in 1986-87, Harper is now merely a steady performer on a juggernaut team—but the role seems to fit him quite nicely.

Harper shot a nifty 52 percent from inside the arc in 1995-96.

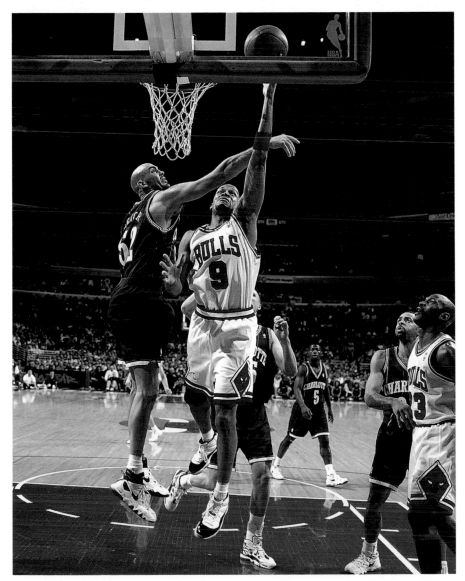

25 STEVE KERR

S ince the NBA began counting long-range jumpers as three points in 1979-80, Steve Kerr has hit them better than anyone else. He shot a nearly unfathomable 52.4 percent (89-of-170) from behind the line in 1994-95, a single-season record and nearly the exact number as his *overall* shooting percentage of 52.7. His bombing average dropped just a tad in 1995-96 to 51.5 (second in the league), but he also hit more of them than ever before—chucking in 122-of-237 to rank second in 3s made on the club to Scottie Pippen despite playing just over 23 minutes per game. At season's end, Kerr had made 48 percent of the 3-pointers he had attempted in his eight-year career.

Anybody who had a chance to see him play in college wouldn't be surprised by this accuracy. A second-team All-American his senior

Kerr's last 407 3-point attempts have resulted in 633 total points.

Despite no starts, Kerr was fifth on the Bulls in minutes played last year.

year at Arizona, he led the 1987-88 Wildcats to the Final Four with a Pac-10-record 57.3 3-point percentage (114-of-199)—capping a great comeback from a severe knee injury that had shelved him the entire previous season.

His specialty makes Kerr quite a valuable asset come crunch time, but the 6'3" guard is by no means a one-dimensional player. He seldom makes mistakes, never gripes about his playing time, is durable (having

appeared in all 82 games three years in a row), and is as hard-working as they come. He does a stellar job running the Bulls' offense coming off the bench, and Phil Jackson likes him enough that he left starter B.J. Armstrong unprotected in the expansion draft to get scooped up by Toronto. Kerr didn't ascend into a starting role himself last year, but he averaged 8.4 points off the bench and scored in double figures an impressive 34 times.

34 BILL WENNINGTON

Basketball big men are like potato chips—it's impossible for NBA coaches to take just one. The Bulls, in fact, liked having seven-footers to throw at opposing centers so much that they stockpiled them like wood for winter during the 1995-96 season, and Bill Wennington was once again among the sturdiest of the bunch. Providing solid backup when Luc Longley was healthy and putting in 20 starts of his own when Luc wasn't, Big Bill turned in his usual serviceable scoring (5.3 points in 15 minutes per game) while leaving the rebounding to Dennis Rodman and others.

Wennington was at his best when starting (7.9 points and 3.3 rebounds per game), which helped the Bulls get through the rough points of the season when Longley and Pippen were ailing and Rodman was up to his usual mischief. Phil Jackson has long felt Bill had the tools to make more of an offensive impact than he has, but Wennington has managed to stretch out his NBA career to nine years wrapped around a pair in Europe

Wennington's 86-percent free-throw shooting led all NBA centers.

from 1991-93. The Montreal native and two-time Olympian has always found a home because of his height, cheerful disposition, and an ability to knock down the 15-footer not often found in men of his latitude.

His talents in the last area were particularly useful during the 1993-94 season, when the Bulls were drastically short in the middle and Wennington averaged 7.1 points and 4.6 rebounds while forcing opposing centers to leave the paint and defend against his jumpers.

A teammate of fellow NBAers Chris Mullin and Walter Berry at St. John's, Wennington helped the Redmen to the Final Four in 1985. Wennington spent five NBA seasons with the Dallas Mavericks, one with the Sacramento Kings, and two in Italy before joining the Bulls.

With Bill in the game, opponents had another potent scorer to worry about.

30 JUD BUECHLER

Professional athletes who spend their time moving from city to city getting work where they can find it are known as "journeymen." Those basketball players whose size makes them too small for certain positions and too big for others are called "tweeners." Those who are both—like Jud Buechler—usually find themselves in trouble.

Entering the 1995-96 season, Buechler had played with four teams in his first five NBA seasons—not even counting the one (Seattle) that originally drafted him out of Arizona and then let him go before he ever suited up. At 6'6", 220 pounds, he wasn't really big enough to be a forward, but he did not really have the speed or skills to play guard at the pro level, either. So he wound up playing a little of both, first in New Jersey, then in San Antonio, then in Golden State, and then in Chicago. Through 1994-95, he owned a scoring average of 4.0 and had earned a reputation as a hard worker who didn't make mistakes (his nickname in college had been "Fundy," for "fundamentals"), but he was never quite good enough to keep around.

In 1995-96, however, the Bulls did keep him around—and Buech-

Buechler gave the Bulls a lift with his fiery spirit and occasional 3s.

Jud netted a season-high 14 points December 9 against Milwaukee.

ler made some solid contributions. The knee problems that had plagued him the year before never resurfaced, and Phil Jackson had him on the floor for an average of 10 minutes in 74 of 82 games. He hit well from outside (40-of-90 3-pointers), scored in double figures six times (including a high of 14), and was used at big guard, small forward, and even power forward in different situations. The California native and off-season beach volleyball player averaged only 3.8 points per game, but no one was complaining—especially Buechler.

RANDY BROWN

On a team with its share of role-players, Randy Brown finished the 1995-96 season ranked last on the Bulls in scoring and rebounds among those appearing in 40 or more games. Yet he still made Chicago's playoff roster for one primary reason: speed. Quick enough to have once snatched six steals in one quarter while with Sacramento, Brown provided a spark off the bench with scrappy defense and an ability to get his hands on the ball.

Hustle has helped the former New Mexico State standout last five years in the NBA despite a 4.7 scoring average. The Bulls signed him as a free agent October 5, 1995, hoping he could give them some quality minutes while Michael Jordan and/or Ron Harper took a breather, and he fit the bill nicely. Appearing in 68 games, he notched 57 steals and 73 assists—respectable figures considering his minutes—and for a bonus added 66 rebounds and 12 blocked shots.

Brown's drive to make the playoff roster included a 16-point, six-steal effort in 21 minutes subbing for Harper against Detroit April 18. And in one February game against the Celtics, Randy made a steal of an inbound pass and then dunked over 6'7" Boston forward Rick Fox. "He really gets after people," remarked Steve Kerr. "That steal and that dunk was probably the play of the year."

Though a low scorer, Brown was one of the best pickpockets in the league.

JAMES EDWARDS

If rookie Jason Caffey represented one end of the Bulls spectrum in 1995-96, James Edwards most certainly occupied the other. The 39-year-old began his NBA career in 1977—when Caffey was four years old—and for most of his 18 seasons with seven teams had provided solid muscle and scoring touch from the low post. A former "Bad Boy" Piston who teamed with Dennis Rodman on Detroit's back-to-back championship clubs of 1989 and 1990, James was reunited with his old teammate when Chicago picked him up just before the 1995-96 season started.

At 7'1", Edwards long posed a problem for other big men with his deft touch on turnaround and fall-away shots. Once past his 36th birthday, however, the problems for defenders began to diminish. After averaging in double figures 13 of

Buddha ranks third all time in seasons played (19) and ninth all time in games played (1,168).

his first 14 seasons, Edwards saw his scoring output drop each season from 13.6 with the Pistons in 1990-91 to 2.7 with the Trail Blazers four years later.

The Bulls were hoping Edwards had a little bit left, but assorted injuries and bouts of ineffectiveness enabled him to see action in just 28 games and shoot 37 percent from the field—a disappointing percentage for a guy who was over 50 percent for his career until very recently. Despite his 3.5 scoring average in 1995-96, he made the playoff roster for primarily the same two reasons he was picked up in the first place: to give six fouls a game to the cause and to help provide some more championship karma to the locker room.

22 JOHN SALLEY

John Salley must have thought he had made a deal with the devil in March 1996. First he was released from the expansion Toronto Raptors (no easy feat) after

an uninspiring 25-game stint (6.0 points, 3.9 rebounds per game), and it appeared his 10-year NBA career might be grinding to a stop. Then he was invited to try out for the big man-desperate Bulls, and he wound up getting a 10-day contract and a chance to join old teammates Dennis Rodman and James Edwards on the best team in the land. It was quite a change of scenery, to be sure, and Salley wound up having his 6'11" body in the right place at the right time in attaining his third championship ring.

Salley had actually worn out his first welcome of the year in the off-

Salley won all three of his NBA titles with Dennis Rodman and James Edwards by his side.

season, when Miami left him unprotected following a 1994-95 campaign in which he had typical Salleyesque stats (7.3 points, 4.5 rebounds per game) but played a brand of ball teammates found uninspiring. This ended a disappointing three-year stint with the Heat in which he never developed into the leader and inside presence Miami coaches had hoped for. But Phil Jackson had no such aspirations. All he wanted was another six fouls to waste on opposing centers and power forwards come playoff time, and in this category Salley has always been willing. By March 23, he was signed through the end of the season, and a few months later he was sizing his finger for another championship ring.

8 DICKEY SIMPKINS

Dickey Simpkins hasn't been what the Bulls had hoped for upon making him their first pick (21st overall) in the 1994 draft, but it may still be too early to make a final assessment on the 24-year-old's talents. He has looked confused and befuddled on the floor some nights, but on others he's shown the moves needed to become a solid power forward.

A largely anonymous player at Providence College, Simpkins was drafted for his defensive potential. He has good size, strength, and quickness to get after NBA forwards, and he runs the floor very well for a big man. Simpkins, though, is a very limited offensive player. He does not possess a great variety of moves in the post and his jump shot

is not a weapon. He simply does not look comfortable with the ball in his hands.

After playing him 586 minutes his rookie season, Phil Jackson gave Dickey just 100 more in 1995-96—but he did make 12 starts in which the Bulls went 10-2. His 3.6 scoring average was almost identical to his 3.5 rookie mark. Rumors had the Bulls shopping Simpkins and his hefty contract just before the trading deadline, and he was cut from the playoff roster once again. Simpkins still has a lot of work to do before he begins to earn more than garbage minutes. Though he'll never be a star, the Bulls hope Dickey can develop into a solid role-player who could provide strong defense and rebounding.

With his strength and quickness, Simpkins packs plenty of potential.

35 JASON CAFFEY

Being a rookie means paying your dues, and pay them is certainly what Jason Caffey did for the Bulls in 1995-96. A surprise pick by Chicago in the first round of the 1995 draft, the 6'8", 255-pounder was counted on to be a bruising power forward. Although Caffey showed flashes of solid play—topped by his 13 points and eight rebounds vs. Cleveland November 15—in the end he was too young and too injured (missing 19 games due to assorted aches and pains) to make much of an impact. He scored just 3.2 points per game while averaging just 9.6 minutes per outing.

The Bulls drafted the long-armed Caffey for his rebounding skills.

Phil Jackson is usually as fair a coach as they come, but he is stubborn on the topic of rookies. Simply put, he does not think they should be put into playoff situations. Perhaps he has grown spoiled viewing the talents of the greatest player in the world on a daily basis, or has memories of a rookie who let him down at a crucial time. In any event, while it appeared Caffey had more athleticism and aggressiveness than some players who did get a shot at the postseason, Jackson reportedly felt the long-armed former Alabama star had not mastered the team offense well enough to warrant a spot on the playoff roster. After a full season of practicing with the greatest team in history, Caffey should step up in 1996-97.

54 JACK HALEY

When this 6'10" journeyman center signed on for his second tour of duty with the Bulls shortly before the start of the 1995-96 season, snickers abounded. The move came just after Chicago traded Will Perdue for Haley's San Antonio teammate and buddy Dennis Rodman, and many felt Haley was brought in simply to keep Dennis out of mischief. Prone to scoring little (3.7 points per game entering 1995-96) and playing even less (108 games over his previous four seasons, including none in 1992-93 due to a knee injury), Haley didn't seem to have much to offer.

By his standards, Jack had a productive preseason (4.8 points per game in under six minutes per contest), but any chance to quiet the skeptics was put on hold when he went on the disabled list with tendinitis in his left knee November 2—the day before the regular season started. He was still in street clothes five months later, but for some reason or another was activated for the final game of the year in time to score five points.

Jack had the best seat in Chicago from which to watch the drive to 70 wins, and he offered an interesting view on the milestone: "This brings an unbelievable amount of gratification. Michael and Scottie and those guys weren't about to cut down the nets. But for guys like Jud Buechler, Steve Kerr, and myself, guys who have traveled around the league, this was a big accomplishment."

Haley played just one game last year—the finale against Washington.

GREATEST TEAM EVER?

Are the Bulls the best in history? Scottie says yes, Wilt says no, and Michael says it's too tough to call.

Asked if the Bulls were the greatest team ever, Michael Jordan shrugged off the question. Others, though, were more opinionated.

The 1995-96 Bulls were the first NBA team to win 70 games in a season. Does that make them the best team ever? Depends on who you ask.

"We've come out and proved to the world that we're the best team of all time," said Scottie Pippen.

"I think my 1985-86 Celtics team could beat them," said broadcaster Danny Ainge.

"The Philadelphia 76ers of 1966-67 were without a doubt the greatest ever," said Wilt Chamberlain.

"The Boston Celtics [of the 1960s] were the greatest team—there's nothing to talk about," said Red Auerbach.

And, of course, we can't forget about the 1971-72 Los Angeles Lakers, who won 69 games including a record 33 in a row.

Here's Michael Jordan's spin on the matter: "I'll never compare teams of different eras, because the game is so different than it was back when the Lakers won 69 games. There are a lot more teams now, but there are a lot more distractions, too. I'm sure there are going to be a lot of doubters no matter how many games we win."

Well, the Bulls won 72, and Michael was right: There are a lot of doubters. A lot of doubters even

though the Bulls set a record by winning 44 consecutive home games (dating back to the 1994-95 season). A lot of doubters even though the Bulls won 33 road games, the most ever in a season by an NBA team. And a lot of doubters even though the Bulls, after pushing their record to 50-6 with a win against Minnesota in February, reached 50 victories with the fewest number of losses faster than any major professional sports team (NBA, NHL, Major League Baseball) this century.

Some naysayers claim that too many of the Bulls' victories came against teams like Minnesota, 98-pound weaklings in a league watered down by three rounds of expansion in eight years. Indeed, the Bulls feasted on the six newer clubs, going 16-4. But hey, they went 56-6 against the rest of the league. Others claim Chicago played most of its games against the inferior Eastern Conference. This is true, and they did feast on the East (47-7), but they also went 25-3

Each of history's three winningest teams had the league's leading rebounder—Wilt Chamberlain for the Lakers and Sixers and Dennis Rodman for the Bulls.

BULLS VS. OTHER GREAT TEAMS

	Record	Points/Game			Reb./Game		Assists/Game		FG Pct.		FT Pct.	
		TOT	OPP	DIF	TOT	OPP	TOT	OPP	TOT	OPP	TOT	OPP
1995-96 Bulls	72-10	105.2	92.9	+12.2	44.6	38.0	24.8	19.4	.478	.448	.746	.717
1971-72 Lakers	69-13	121.0	108.7	+12.3	56.4	52.3	27.2	24.3	.490	.432	.734	.768
1966-67 76ers	68-13	125.2	115.8	+9.4	70.4	NA	26.4	NA	.483	NA	.680	NA
1985-86 Celtics	67-15	114.1	104.7	+9.4	46.4	41.5	29.1	23.5	.508	.461	.794	.748

against the West, which featured powerhouses Seattle, San Antonio, and Utah—not to mention Olajuwon's Rockets, Magic's Lakers, and Barkley's Suns.

While some claim that teams have it easier these days—better medical care, posh hotels, private planes instead of charters—this did not give the Bulls any edge over their opponents, who were equally well cared for. In reality, the Bulls were at a *disadvantage* because they had to overcome the "distractions" Jordan was talking about. While Chicago's opponents may have chatted with a few reporters before games, the Bulls were suffocated by media hordes, inundated with requests for appearances, and swarmed by autograph hounds. When they drove 90 miles by bus to Milwaukee for victory No. 70, a news chopper hovered above every inch of the way. Wilt's Lakers never experienced such pressure.

This is not to say the Bulls were far and away the greatest team in basketball history. Three aforementioned teams—the 1971-72 Lakers, 1966-67 76ers, and 1985-86 Celtics—can all make legitimate claims to being history's best.

Statistically, the Lakers were the greatest team ever. They made 49.0 percent of their field-goal attempts while holding their opponents to 43.2 percent, a differential nearly twice as great as what the Bulls accomplished in 1995-96. The Lakers led the NBA in rebounding by a

Though Wilt Chamberlain (headband) led the 1971-72 Lakers to 33 straight wins, he said they weren't as good as his 1966-67 76ers.

wide margin and outscored their foes by 1,007 points (compared to 1,004 for the Bulls). Chamberlain led the league in shooting accuracy and rebounding, Jerry West led it in assists, and West and Gail Goodrich both averaged more than 25 points a game. And the Lakers won 33 straight games (the Bulls' longest streak was 18).

Chamberlain's argument that his Sixers actually were better than his

1971-72 Lakers is supported by the level of competition in 1966-67. Only 10 teams composed the NBA that year, and competition was so fierce that the St. Louis Hawks—with Lou Hudson, Bill Bridges, Lenny Wilkens, Joe Caldwell, Richie Guerin, Zelmo Beaty, and Paul Silas—lost more games than they won.

The Sixers had no weak links. Chamberlain (24.1 points and 24.2

rebounds per game), Luke Jackson, and Chet Walker composed a granite wall up front, and Hal Greer and Wally Jones were rock solid in the backcourt. The sixth man was Hall of Famer Billy Cunningham. The Sixers started 46-4 before coasting to the finish line at 68-14.

Ainge's 1985-86 Celtics lacked the consistency of the 1971-72 Lakers and the overwhelming strength of the 1966-67 Sixers, but no team (including the Bulls) has ever been better at home. Including playoff games, the Celtics were 50-1 at Boston Garden.

The Celtics featured a front line of Larry Bird, Robert Parish, and Kevin McHale, with Dennis Johnson in the backcourt and Bill Walton coming off the bench. They absolutely toyed with their opponents. Occasionally they'd take a night off (10 of their 15 losses came against teams with losing records), but they proved themselves against the best, going 7-0 against Milwaukee and the Lakers, the second- and third-best teams in the league, and posted a sterling 15-3 mark in the postseason.

Despite the accomplishments of these three clubs, critics can poke holes in all of them. First of all, the Lakers: While some dis the Bulls for playing in a watered-down league—there were 29 NBA teams in 1995-96 compared to only 17 when the Lakers played—one must remember that the 11-team American Basketball Association was around in 1971-72, draining a lot of the talent out of the NBA.

Though the ABA didn't exist when the Sixers played, and though there were only 10 NBA teams then, the athletic ability of NBA players in 1966 just doesn't compare to those in 1996. The average player in 1966-67 was 1½ inches shorter and, more importantly, lacked the quickness and leaping ability of players today. People did not take off at the free-throw line and dunk like Jordan and Pippen,

and there weren't any 6'10" guys who could man the point like Toni Kukoc.

Shooting has improved since then. Teams shot 44.1 percent from the field in 1966-67 compared to 46.2 in 1995-96—and 20 percent of the shots last year were 3-point bombs. The fact that the average 3-point percentage jumped from 28.0 in 1979-80 to 33.3 in 1993-94 indicates that shooting has become more refined.

As for the Celtics, their 15 losses were 50 percent more than the Bulls'. They were very beatable on the road (27-14), and they outscored opponents by just 9.4 points per game (compared to 12.3 for the Lakers, 12.2 for the Bulls, and 9.4 for the Sixers).

The 1966-67 Sixers featured four future NBA head coaches, including Bob Weiss (left) and Matt Guokas (to Weiss's left).

No one will ever know who was the greatest team in basketball history, but one could justifiably pick the Bulls for three simple reasons:
1) They won more games than anyone else.
2) They did it under unprecedented pressure.
3) The talent level in the NBA is greater now than in previous decades.

Pippen, for one, would love to put an end to all the debates. Said Pip of the 1971-72 Lakers: "If they want to meet us on the court tomorrow, let's get it on."

HOOPLA!

Jay Leno, Oprah Winfrey, Madonna, the Red Hot Chili Peppers.... Everyone's caught up in Bulls mania!

A highway drive covered live via helicopter, complete with folks crowding overpasses to wave and cheer the travelers on. Interviews with Ted Koppel on *Nightline.* Book-signings, famous hairdos, and fanatics brawling it out—just for a chance to pay and see them perform.

The O.J. Simpson Bronco chase? Hillary Rodham Clinton's latest goodwill tour? A Michael Jackson concert? None of the above. In fact, this list of wild and woolly events is nothing more than a few random incidents in the lives of the 1995-96 Chicago Bulls.

"It's a season above and beyond the normal," said coach Phil Jackson, and no one would argue the point. Basketball god Michael Jordan, exterior decorator Dennis Rodman, and the rest of their mates did more than go 72-10 during the 1995-96 season; they became a national phenomenon.

Below: During his weeklong visit to Chicago, Jay Leno welcomed guests Scottie Pippen and Michael Jordan as well as the Dancing Rodmans. Right: One of the Bulls' mascots attempts the trampoline slam.

Top left: *Four guys fall woefully short in their impersonation of Dennis Rodman.* **Bottom left:** *Several days after breaking down in tears on* Oprah, *Rodman gave Winfrey his jersey after a playoff game.*

Sparked by a 10-1 start, the Bulls became the greatest ongoing public relations event the league had ever seen. Reemerging as the game's greatest star, Jordan was once again showing up regularly on ESPN's *SportsCenter* as well as in commercials for soda, underwear, and sneakers. Jordan once again adorned magazine covers with a basketball rather than a baseball bat, which was a welcome sight for fans and NBA merchandisers alike.

When Magic Johnson announced his return to the league after nearly five years of retirement, it seemed only fitting that one of his first opponents be Michael Jordan. For one glorious night in Los Angeles in early February, the clock was turned back, all was right with the world, and courtside seats were going for $3,000 a pop.

After the Lakers game, the Bulls were an absurd 41-3. And with homecourt advantage throughout the playoffs all but a certainty, Chicagoans now had only two things on their minds: Could the Bulls supplant the 1972-73 Lakers (69-13) as the winningest team in NBA history, and what color will Dennis's hair be tomorrow?

Rodman was now the NBA's greatest sideshow, especially after he started giving away his jersey after games. Rodman's new hobby led to the unveiling of some creative banners at Chicago's United Center. Among the best were waved by a fan from afar ("Mr. Rodman—I Came From Venezuela To Get Your Jersey") and four women with pink hair ("We're Tickled Pink 4 Rodman"). One gentleman, not worrying about being blunt, held up a placard reading: "Rodman, Gimme The Damn Shirt."

On the sign: 70 [Bulls logo]

$23 + 33 +$
$91 + 7 = 70$

Th[e]
winni[ng]
equation

CHICAGO
BULLS
"70" IS

Above: *Thousands of Bulls fans infiltrated Milwaukee's Bradley Center April 16 in hopes of seeing win No. 70.* **Right:** *"No. 23" wasn't the only hot-selling jersey.*

The *Chicago Tribune* reported that Rodman had "evolved into something of a merchandising machine in Chicago." And while Jordan was still way ahead in mass appeal, Dennis had moved past teammates Scottie Pippen and Toni Kukoc in replica jersey sales. The NBA does not furnish statistics on merchandise sales of individual teams, but *Sports Illustrated* stated that the Bulls had accounted for as

began popping up on playgrounds and in classrooms throughout the country. Even after Rodman finally blew his fuse March 16 and was suspended six games for head-butting referee Ted Bernhardt, No. 91 jerseys kept flying off shelves. Dennis made a deal with the band Red Hot Chili Peppers in which he exchanged jerseys for front-row seats to their Chicago concert; the band members ended up wearing the jerseys on stage. It became obvious that Bulls Fever had reached a new level when a 3.8-point scorer was lauded with the cardboard request: "Jud Buechler, Can I Have Your Jersey Please?"

One United Center promotion proved so popular that McDonald's made it a regular item in Chicago-area stores. When they ordered a large soda, patrons could get their very own Rodman cup—which featured four different front-and-rear head shots of Dennis that changed hair color as the cup was cooled or heated. A huge mural of Rodman adorning the side of a building stopped so much highway traffic that it had to be painted over. And when Madonna's ex released his autobiography, *Bad as I Wanna Be,* during the playoffs, he showed up for a book-signing wearing skintight pants, drag queen makeup, and a pink boa. Among the book's revelations: "The NBA is afraid of me" and "I fantasize about being with another man."

The Bulls also went through the entire season sold out at home, giving them a string of 344 consecutive regular-season home sellouts dating back to 1987-88. Just as the Los Angeles Forum was the place to see and be seen during the 1980s, the United Center—while lacking the dirty, dingy charm and fans-on-top-of-you atmosphere of old Chicago Stadium—had become the "in" arena of the '90s. Oprah Winfrey, Jesse Jackson, Jay Leno, Gene Siskel, John Cusack, Charlie Sheen, and Bill Murray were among the

Top: *The Rodman mural near the Kennedy Expressway was removed because of too many gawkers.* **Bottom:** *Rodman's hair on his McDonald's cups changed colors depending on the temperature of the liquid.*

much as 40 percent of the $3 billion in merchandising sales generated by the NBA in 1995.

Bulls Mania stretched all the way to the West Coast. A riot nearly ensued at the February 1 game in Sacramento when thousands of fans—most of whom had waited all night—clashed outside Arco Arena in pursuit of the few hundred remaining standing-room-only tickets to the Bulls-Kings contest. The next night in Los Angeles, the "Michael and Magic Show" drew its $3,000 courtside offers. And on February 4 in Denver, ticket brokers were commanding $425 for choice seats to the Bulls-Nuggets battle—a record for the city surpassing the $400 country crooner Garth Brooks commanded in 1992.

As the early months of 1996 passed and the team record grew (54-6 on March 7), more and more black, red, and white paraphernalia

Actors Charlie Sheen (left) and John Cusack scammed courtside seats for a Bulls game. Cusack was born in Evanston, a Chicago suburb.

celebrities spotted at games during the regular season and playoffs. Even film directors Spike Lee and Woody Allen came by when not watching the Knicks from their courtside seats at Madison Square Garden.

Honors and publicity for the team came in all forms. Pippen appeared in an episode of *E.R.* in February, then in April threw out the first ball at the White Sox home opener. Rodman appeared in *Playboy,* and movie critic Siskel proved such a big fan that he did a piece for

Chicago's Channel 2 news in which he compared members of the Bulls to the characters in the film *Legends of the Fall.*

The hype reached its peak on April 16, the day the 69-9 Bulls stood poised to break the record at Milwaukee. Channel 2 assigned its "Chopper 2" helicopter to follow the team bus and offer live feeds of its 90-mile drive to Wisconsin, while weathermen compared the record-setting 70 wins to the 70 degrees anticipated for the next day's forecast.

After the record became reality with an 86-80 win over the Bucks, Ted Koppel and his *Nightline* crew devoted their entire ABC broadcast to the team. Ted spent part of the

show interviewing Bulls superfans. When one fanatic was asked by Koppel, "Do you ever do anything but worry about the Bulls?", he answered in a straight face befitting a Middle Eastern diplomat, "Well, not really."

Leno spent an entire week airing his *Tonight Show* from Chicago. Jay drove the audience into wild hysterics on opening night, when he replaced his ever-popular Dancing Itos with the Dancing Rodmans—who came out with No. 91 jerseys and glow-in-the-dark hair.

But perhaps nothing provided a better example of the fine line separating the Bulls as a sports franchise from that of a national phenomenon than a small error in a wire-service story that ran uncaught in many papers across the country. It identified the First Lady of the United States: Hillary Rodman Clinton.

So intoxicating was Bulls mania that a fan was touting Jud Buechler for President of the United States.

FOUR UP, FOUR DOWN

The Bulls charge past their four playoff opponents en route to their fourth NBA title.

Despite all the attention Chicago received for its landmark 72 wins, the euphoria surrounding the accomplishment quickly evaporated when the postseason began. The playoffs haven't always been kind to regular-season heroes, and the basketball history books are filled with stories of great teams that failed miserably in their quest to win the title.

The Bulls didn't want to replicate the collapse of the 1972-73 Boston Celtics, who won 68 regular-season games before falling apart against New York in the Eastern Conference finals.

"(Winning 72 games) puts us in a position where there's a little more pressure on us," Bulls forward Scottie Pippen said. "Everybody expects us to win the championship. We've proven all season that no team can dominate us. Now, we have to prove it again."

For the 1995-96 season to be something that belonged in storybooks as well as almanacs, the Bulls would have to add 15 more wins to their 72.

"I've said many times that we did not start out the season looking to win 70 games," Michael Jordan said after the team beat Milwaukee for No. 70. "We set out to win a championship, and that's our focus now."

Above: *Derek Harper's Knicks couldn't keep up with the big boys.* Right: *Dennis Rodman senses ultimate victory during a Game 1 rout of Orlando.*

CHICAGO TURNS OFF THE HEAT

Even in the lightning-fast world of first-round mini-series blowouts, there is always the opportunity for a little controversy. The Bulls may have dispatched Miami in three short games, but they didn't get away cleanly. By the time Chicago moved on to its date with New York, Jordan had survived a bad back, Dennis Rodman had been ejected, and several Bulls had engaged Heat center Alonzo Mourning in trash talk. Nobody said the road to the title was going to be a dull one.

Even though the Heat had dealt the Bulls one of their 10 regular-season losses, they provided little competition in the playoffs. Chicago started slowly in Game 1, but—behind Jordan's 35 points—pulled away for a 102-85 win. A riled Mourning fouled out, Heat coach Pat Riley was ejected, and it was clear that Miami was as over-matched as an eighth-seeded team should be.

"We sensed the kill when we started this series," Pippen said.

The Bulls' 106-75 second-game rout was filled with interesting sub-plots. Jordan suffered a back injury in the second quarter but returned to play the third period. He finished with 29 points despite lingering back spasms.

While Jordan ached, Rodman misbehaved. Late in the third, he picked up his second technical foul of the game and was banished to the locker room. Though he in-flicted no bodily harm on the refer-ees and kept his histrionics to a minimum, The Worm provided the Bulls with some unneeded worries. Jackson called the incident "embar-

rassing," and some Bulls wondered whether Rodman was headed for a playoff meltdown similar to the one he suffered the previous season with San Antonio.

Just as back spasms and petu-lance couldn't stop the Bulls in the second game, they were not a fac-tor in the deciding contest. Neither

Above: *Michael Jordan stretches out his aching back during Game 3 vs. Miami. Despite the pain, MJ averaged his cus-tomary 30 points a game for the series.* **Left:** *With defense like this from Scot-tie Pippen, Chris Gatling and the Heat could muster only 75 points in Game 2. They aver-aged just 83.7 points per game and shot a miser-able 42.1 percent from the field.*

was Miami. Despite having to lie on his stomach next to the Bulls' bench and stretch his back when he wasn't playing, Jordan scored 26, including 14 in a decisive first quarter. Pippen added a triple-double that included 22 points, 18 rebounds, and 11 as-sists. Chicago won 112-91. The Knicks were next.

BULLS KNOCK OUT KNICKS IN FIVE

The New York Knicks entered their second-round series with the Bulls like an aging heavyweight looking for one last shot at redemption. Once considered destined to win an NBA title, the Knicks were slipping. Sure, the familiar names were still there—Ewing, Harper, Starks, Oakley, Mason—but the team lacked the same fire and hardly inspired the same fear as it did a few years back.

It was no surprise, then, that the Bulls dispatched New York in five games, even though it wasn't a particularly attractive triumph. The Bulls relied too much on Jordan, thanks to Pippen's weak play in the first four games and a back injury to Toni Kukoc, who missed the final three. It just placed more pressure on Michael, who dominated.

"I find myself bailing the team out," Jordan said after his magnifi-

Bill Wennington's slam and jumper in the final 1:28 of Game 4 helped Chicago pull out a 94-91 victory.

cent 46-point effort wasn't enough to subdue the Knicks in the third game. "I have taken a lot of shots. That's a good sign of us not executing our offense."

It was the Knicks who failed to execute during the first two games of the series at the United Center. They had chances to win both contests but faltered in the fourth quarter in both instances. The first game was particularly frustrating for the Knicks. With Pippen, Ron Harper, Luc Longley, and Kukoc shooting well below 50 percent from the field, all the Bulls had was Jordan, still stiff and sore from his back injury. That couldn't prevent him from finishing with 44 points. "I don't want to come out looking hurt,"

Forced to do it all in Game 3, Michael Jordan shot left-handed over Patrick Ewing for two of his 46.

In Game 1, Ron Harper and the Bulls blanketed John Starks, who went 0-for-9 from the field.

Jordan said. "If they see you bleed, they'll go after the blood." With 4:07 remaining, the Knicks had closed to within one, 83-82. But missed shots, turnovers, and poor decisions sabotaged New York, which fell 91-84 to a very beatable team.

"This would have been a good day to jump on us," Jordan said. "Scottie had an off day. Harper did nothing offensively. Toni couldn't give us anything, either. I was the only guy doing anything offensively. Yes, they could have gotten us easy."

The Knicks couldn't get the Bulls in the second game, either. With 10 minutes left, New York was within a point but allowed Chicago to embark on a 12-0 run that put the game away. The final was 91-80, and again Jordan carried the load. He scored 28 points, and though Pippen added 19, he did so on 7-for-21 shooting. Knicks guard John Starks was unable to match his big talk with big play and finished the two-game stretch shooting just 2-for-14 from the field. The Bulls

were up 2-0, and the Knicks were frustrated.

"Both games, we had the opportunity to win," New York center Patrick Ewing said. "We had them where we wanted them and let it slip away in the fourth quarter. I'm angry. We're angry. We should've won. We could've won, but we didn't. We still feel we're capable of beating this team."

The Knicks were right, and they proved it in Game 3 at Madison Square Garden. Despite Jordan's 46-point salvo, which included two late 3-point bombs that forced overtime, the Knicks gained some hope with a 102-99 overtime win, proving that even Jordan can't win every game by himself.

He didn't have to do that in Game 4, just 24 hours later. Bill Wennington, of all people, provided a boost with four late-game points, and the Bulls took a 3-1 series lead with a 94-91 win. Though Jordan scored 27 points, he did so

on 7-for-23 shooting and was drained from his Game 3 heroics. It didn't matter. The Bulls grabbed a huge rebounding advantage, including a 23-4 edge on the offensive glass. It seemed as if everybody contributed. Even little-used guard Randy Brown scored eight points.

"We knew we had to have someone step up," coach Jackson said. "Michael did not have the energy to play the game at the level he had (in Game 3). He knew it and I knew it. Our bench did a great job."

The fifth game, a 94-81 Bulls win, was anticlimactic, although a strong performance from Pippen made news. He had 15 points and 11 rebounds to go with 35 points for Jordan, who averaged 36 for the series. The Knicks were done. Up next was the long-awaited rematch with Orlando.

Dennis Rodman bends over backwards for a rebound. He averaged 15.6 for the series.

Poof! Magic Disappear in Four

It wasn't supposed to be this easy. While the NBA and its assorted marketing partners hunkered down for a presumed marquee matchup between the league's hottest old and new commodities, the Bulls used four games to display the yawning gap between experience and potential. Orlando never had a chance in the Eastern Conference finals and ended up on the business end of a Chicago broom that swept it away from the playoffs with seeming ease.

Unlike the 1994-95 season, when the Bulls struggled to find continuity and focus in the conference semis and lost to the Magic in six games, Chicago entered this series with Orlando with a clear sense of purpose—not to mention a full-force Jordan. The results were resounding. Chicago dominated the Magic and blasted into the NBA Finals. The Magic were left to ponder just how they would close the gap.

"Michael Jordan told me, 'Remember, it took me forever to get over the hump,'" Magic forward Dennis Scott told *USA Today* after the series clincher. "He told me all about how Detroit used to kick his butt, and how long it took him to do it. When we were in Toronto during the regular season, Isiah Thomas told us the same thing. It was Boston that kept killing (the Pistons). Now, we're going through it. We're trying to get over the hump. The only thing is, this is a mighty big hump."

And how. Whenever Orlando thought it might be close to exerting its will over the Bulls, Chicago re-

Scottie Pippen (18 points) was one of six Bulls in double figures in a 121-83 Game 1 blowout.

sponded. In the series' second game, that meant overcoming an 18-point third-quarter deficit. In the finale, it was a case of erasing an 11-point first-half margin and a nine-point shortfall in the third period. Though many teams had wilted against Orlando during the regular season, Chicago seemed to get stronger when the adversity mounted.

"This team is so tight," Rodman said after the fourth game. "We have guys with a desire to win, who won't let you kick our butt. We're all about being precise. We're all about one mind, one goal. It's like in the third quarter today, when we

Chicago tallied an incredible 45 steals during the series, leading to a ton of fastbreak points.

Chicago defense that chose not to double-team him, Orlando's other players were almost invisible. Compounding matters was a serious elbow injury suffered by power forward Horace Grant that would sideline him for the entire series.

"I couldn't believe it," Magic reserve guard Donald Royal said after the game. "The hunger was in their eyes, and we were like a team just happy to be here, as opposed to one that is the defending conference champion."

If Royal was incredulous after Game 1, he had to be in shock after the Bulls staged a remarkable comeback to take a 2-0 series lead. The Magic bolted to a 53-38 halftime lead in Game 2 on the strength of 26 points by O'Neal, and they extended the advantage to 18 early in

the third period. They collapsed quickly after that. Jordan scored 17 points in the quarter and keyed a 21-5 run that brought Chicago back within two, 69-67. From then on, it was a case of the Bulls' defense strangling the Magic and securing a 93-88 win.

Orlando turned over the ball repeatedly in the second half and was unable to get the ball to either of its stars—O'Neal or Hardaway—consistently. The Magic were hurt by another sorry effort by Scott, who scored a quiet 13 points after being shut out in the first game. Jordan, meanwhile, finished with 35, while Pippen added 17 points, 10 boards,

Toni Kukoc, who racked up 10 assists in Game 1, splits Brian Shaw and Jon Koncak with a pass.

knew we were about to take over. We didn't say a thing. We didn't have to say anything. We knew it. We could see it in Orlando's eyes."

There was no need for a dramatic coming together in the first game of the series. Chicago, which had seemed somewhat vulnerable against the Knicks, blasted to a 121-83 victory. The Bulls put six players in double figures, led by Jordan's 21, and obliterated Orlando on the backboards, 62-28, with Rodman's 21 leading the way. Although Magic guard Anfernee Hardaway had a spectacular afternoon, with 38 points on 15-for-21 shooting, and center Shaquille O'Neal scored a relatively quiet 27 against a

and nine assists. Rodman, for whom scoring was a mere afterthought for much of the year, picked up 15 points to go with his dozen rebounds.

"Orlando came out in the first half and made all the right adjustments from Game 1," Jordan said after the game. "We had to go into halftime and make the right adjustments so we could get back into the game. We found a weakness, and we said, 'Let's attack this weakness.' We said, 'Let's keep the pressure on until they prove that they can stop, change, or alter.' They never did."

Though the Magic headed back to Orlando with some hope, it was clear the Bulls were the better team, particularly with Grant (the only Magic player with a championship ring) sidelined. If the home court was supposed to help boost the Magic's performance, it sure didn't in Game 3. Chicago blasted past its host 86-67, thoroughly stifling the Orlando offense and leaving little

doubt that it was operating on a much higher level than its rival. The Magic's dismal 34-percent shooting included only 22 percent from beyond the 3-point arc. Though Orlando cut Chicago's lead to six after

The lucky Bulls fans who made it to Orlando enjoyed sunshine, Disney World, and a four-game sweep.

three quarters, it mustered only two points in the first 8:16 of the fourth. The end was near.

Orlando gained points for a stout effort in its 106-101 Game 4 loss, particularly since it was without Grant, guard Nick Anderson, and reserve backcourt performer Brian Shaw. The Magic held a 56-47 halftime lead but wilted under another second-half Chicago comeback that included healthy portions of Jordan's magic. Despite playing on a tender ankle, Jordan finished with 45 points on 16-for-23 shooting and appeared as if 50 or 60 were not out of the question. Orlando had acquitted itself well in the final game of the series. Jordan was just better.

"We are fortunate this afternoon to ride on the coattails of Michael Jordan," Jackson said. "We were watching him closely. He did not feel well today coming into the game. He rolled his ankle the other day.

"But Michael Jordan has a penchant for coming up with these kind of games under duress."

Luc Longley takes Anthony Bonner to school in Game 3.

BULLS SLAM SONICS FOR TITLE NO. 4

Despite 72 regular-season wins and three playoff series triumphs, the Bulls approached their NBA Finals date with Seattle as if they had accomplished nothing. And, for many, a Finals flop against the younger SuperSonics would have rendered the 1995-96 season largely unfulfilled, no matter what had preceded it.

The oddsmakers weren't exactly worried and made the Bulls prohibitive 8:1 favorites to take the title. But since no one in Las Vegas has ever won an NBA title, players and coaches didn't pay too much attention to the odds.

"Yeah, I think we can win this series," Seattle coach George Karl said. "I'm a little taken aback by some of the talk I'm hearing. Do I think they have a great team? Yes, they have a great team. But we can beat them."

Most believed the series was all about team defense. Both teams had proven themselves highly skilled in disrupting opponents' attacks throughout the year, particularly in the halfcourt. Chicago had dismantled Orlando with a fierce, trapping strategy, while Seattle had thrived all year thanks to a borderline zone concept that kept rivals from developing any offensive rhythms.

"You don't play defense, you don't win championships," Jordan said before the series. His rivals agreed.

Hersey Hawkins (left), Gary Payton, Detlef Schrempf, and others tried to guard Michael Jordan, but no one could handle the master.

"When I'm behind, I coach defense," Karl said. "You have to control the game to get back in it, and you can only do that at the defensive end."

The Bulls enjoyed eight days of rest before finally facing the Sonics (who needed seven games to defeat Utah). Jordan overcame a battalion of defenders to score a "quiet" 28 points in the opener, but it was Kukoc's 10 straight points at the

beginning of the fourth quarter that propelled the Bulls to a 107-90 victory.

Seattle stayed close through the first three quarters of Game 1 and trailed only 79-77 after three. But Kukoc and the trademark stifling Bulls defense propelled Chicago to victory. The Sonics, who had scored a total of 59 points in the second and third quarters, were held to just 13 in the final 12 minutes.

Although the Bulls made just 43.0 percent of their field goals, they committed only seven turnovers against the vaunted Sonic defense and forced Seattle into 18 giveaways. Pippen scored 21 points, Kukoc added 18, Harper had 15, and Longley tallied 14.

"We were out of synch a little bit offensively," Jordan said. "That's natural for having eight days off. I think the guys really had the determination to come out and run hard and play hard."

The final margin may have been 17, but Seattle didn't give up easily. The Sonics matched the Bulls shot-for-shot and elbow-for-elbow in the physical, at times antagonistic, game (Sonic Frank Brickowski was ejected for skirmishing with Rodman). Seattle received a tremendous performance from Shawn Kemp, who scored 32 points on 9-of-14 shooting. He, however, was the lone offensive standout for the Sonics, who shot just 39.7 percent from the field.

If the Sonics were going to win even one against the Bulls, they blew their chance in Game 2, when Chicago sputtered on offense. The Bulls went without a field goal for the final six minutes, yet they still earned a 92-88 victory that gave them a commanding 2-0 lead.

"Chicago did what it had to do; kept the homecourt advantage," Karl said. "But I don't think we worry about anything but the third game. There's still good stuff out there to learn from. . . . They've got two wins, but we've learned."

What the Sonics learned most in Game 2 was that even when Jordan is "held" to 29 points, Chicago has several other weapons capable of detonating. In this particular instance, it was Rodman who exploded—in a good way. The Worm grabbed a game-high 20 rebounds,

In Game 2, Seattle star Shawn Kemp managed only 14 points in 42 minutes, thanks to Luc Longley and the Bulls' relentless defense.

The 6'10" Toni Kukoc started at guard in Game 3 for the ailing Ron Harper and created an assortment of mismatch problems for Seattle.

11 offensive, on a night when Chicago shot just 30-for-77 from the field.

"I give Dennis a lot of credit," Jordan said. "I think he came in with a lot of heart, especially down the stretch."

Though the Bulls' offense continued to sputter, their trusty defense was again rock solid. Seattle made just 41.3 percent of its shots from the field and committed 16 turnovers. Point guard Gary Payton managed only 13 and lacked his usual brashness. He and Jordan even staged a little trash-talking summit late in the game, and the veteran Chicago guard appeared to get the better of that exchange, too.

The Sonics desperately needed a killer instinct in Game 3 at Key Arena, but it was the Bulls who wielded the knives. With Jordan at

peak performance, Chicago bolted to a 34-16 first-quarter lead en route to a 108-86 cakewalk and a 3-0 series lead.

"That's the first time I've seen Chicago with killer eyes in the series," Karl said. "I saw a team that wasn't going to lose. . . . They had a mentality and an edge we didn't have."

Jordan scored 12 points in the first quarter of Game 3 and erupted

for 15 in a row in the second. The Chicago guard blew past every double-team and tortured those assigned to guard him one-on-one. He finished with 36 points.

There were some interesting subplots beneath Jordan's outburst. Chicago started Kukoc at guard, since Harper was troubled by a bad knee, and the switch caused significant matchup problems for Seattle. The Sonics used forward Detlef Schrempf on Kukoc, instead of on Jordan, as they had in the first two games. Kukoc finished with 14 points. Seattle couldn't handle Longley, either. The big Aussie scored 19.

Despite 19 points of his own, Payton was again frustrated by a Chicago defense designed to keep him from penetrating. "They're throwing everything at me," he said. "They're figuring that if you can stop me from doing a lot of things, it will neutralize our team a lot."

The odds of Seattle winning this series were now infinitesimal. In the 50-year history of NBA playoffs, 50 teams had been down 3-0 in a series and zero had come back to win. The Sonics, though, were determined to avoid the broom.

Backed by raucous fans and a what-do-we-got-to-lose? attitude, Seattle busted out in Game 4 to a 53-32 lead at the half. All of the club's big guns—Kemp, Payton, Schrempf, and Hersey Hawkins— were smoking, and the Sonics

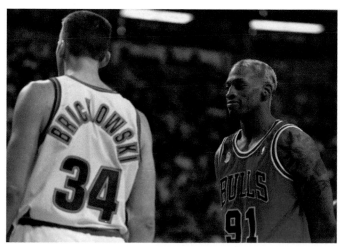

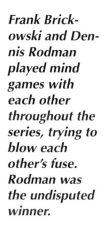

Frank Brickowski and Dennis Rodman played mind games with each other throughout the series, trying to blow each other's fuse. Rodman was the undisputed winner.

drained 7-of-13 3-pointers in the half. "I told the team, 'I'd rather see you play crazy and out of control than the way you were playing,'" Karl said. "We played a great first half and we were aggressive."

The Bulls, meanwhile, were putrid in the first 24 minutes. Jordan and Pippen threw up mostly bricks, Harper limped along on his gimpy knee, and the team shot just 1-of-8 from 3-point land.

The Bulls cut the lead to 13 in the third quarter but couldn't make any real headway. The lead remained 21 after three quarters and again after four, 107-86. Kemp led with 25, including a reverse jam in which he wound up sitting on Rodman's shoulders. Jordan (6-of-19, 23 points) and Pippen (4-of-17, nine points) were anxious for Game 5.

But the fifth contest, also in Seattle, seemed like an extension of Game 4, as Kemp, Hawkins, and Payton pushed Seattle to a 39-34 lead. For Chicago, a hobbled Pippen (ankle and knee) again had trouble shooting, and no Bull could can a 3. A rejuvenated Jordan kept the Bulls in the game, scoring 11 in the second period including two on a spectacular breakaway drive. The Sonics led at the half 43-42.

Seattle clung to a 62-60 advantage after three, but inept 3-point shooting was just killing the Bulls—they missed 20 straight at one point—and the Sonics moved out to a 82-69 lead. Treys by Pippen and Kerr gave Chicagoans some hope (84-77), but free throws sealed it for Seattle, 89-78.

Jordan scored 26 in Game 5 but only two in the fourth quarter. Pippen made just 5-of-20 shots.

"It was obviously our shooting," Jackson said. "We just couldn't knock our shots down."

Even though Game 6 was in Chicago, the Bulls were not necessarily the favorites—not with the Sonics' confidence soaring and Pippen's and Harper's health in doubt. Scottie and Ronnie, though, seemed

The Bulls' long-armed defense fenced off Seattle's Gary Payton early in the series, but the point guard found the magic in Games 4 and 5.

at full strength in the first quarter—exemplified by an early Pippen steal that led to a Harper jumper.

Pippen, in fact, had four first-half steals. Backed by an especially vocal crowd, the Bulls played passionately on defense, outworked Seattle on the boards, and took a 45-38 halftime lead. Jordan, with his sons waving a "Happy Father's Day" poster, had 14 points.

The lead remained seven until Chicago went on a quick and explosive 12-2 run. A 3-pointer by Harper, a tip-in and three-point play by Rodman, and a lay-in by Jordan put the Bulls ahead 64-47. Seattle answered with nine straight, and the third quarter ended 67-58.

When Kukoc canned two treys

early in the fourth, and with a jacked-up Rodman grabbing every rebound in sight, the long-awaited celebration seemed imminent. Kemp fouled out with more than four minutes to go, and a Pippen 3 put Chicago up 82-66. Soon it was over, 87-75, and Jordan lay on the floor, hugging the ball, mobbed by teammates and with the din of hysterical fans in his ears. Jordan, the Finals' MVP, ran to the locker room and sobbed on the floor, undoubtedly moved on this Father's Day by the memory of his late dad, James.

"I can't even put it into words," a shaky Jordan said immediately afterwards. "This is special because this is for my father on Father's Day. That means a lot to me."

Photo credits:

Front cover: **NBA Photos:** Nathaniel S. Butler (left); Barry Gossage (center); Scott Cunningham (right).

Back cover: **Andrew D. Bernstein/NBA Photos.**

Allsport USA: 92, 93, 94; **AP/Wide World Photos:** 30 (bottom); Fred Jewell: 80 (bottom); Beth A. Keiser: 50, 54; Jeffrey Phelps: credits page; 81 (top); Susan Ragan: 44 (left); Todd Rosenberg: 60 (bottom); John Swart: 47; Phil Velasquez/Chicago Sun-Times: 86 (top); **Bettmann Archive:** 28, 33, 74, 76; Corbis: 77; **Focus on Sports:** 48; Jerry Waghte: 25; **Mathew Hohmann:** 82 (bottom); **Chuck Kuhn/Shooting Star:** 24 (bottom); **NBA Photos:** contents (bottom center); Ray Amati: 81 (bottom); Bill Baptist: 66 (bottom); Andrew D. Bernstein: 13, 19 (right), 22, 27, 29, 30 (top), 31, 34, 37 (top), 52, 62, 67 (top), 83 (top), 85, 96; Nathaniel S. Butler: title page, contents (top left & bottom right); 9 (top), 14, 16, 20 (top), 21, 36, 40, 41, 42, 45, 46, 49, 53 (bottom), 56, 75, 79, 86 (bottom), 88 (top), 95; Chris Covatta: 60 (top); Scott Cunningham: contents (bottom left), 9 (bottom), 17, 20 (bottom), 24 (top), 38, 39, 43 (bottom), 53 (top), 55, 58, 61, 64, 65, 66 (top), 68 (bottom), 71 (bottom), 72 (top), 73, 83 (bottom); Gary Dineen: 6, 70 (bottom), 80 (top); Garrett Ellwood: 91 (top); Sam Forencich: 57; Barry Gossage: contents (top center & top right), 11, 18, 23, 51, 67 (bottom), 68 (top), 69 (top), 70 (top), 71 (top), 89 (bottom), 90, 91 (bottom); Andy Hayt: 8; Fernando Medina: 10; Layne Murdoch: 72 (bottom); Noren Trotman: 7, 12, 15, 59, 63, 69 (bottom), 84, 87, 88 (bottom); Rocky Widner: 19 (left); **NBC Photo by Margaret Norton:** 78; **Retna Ltd.:** Sue Ogrocki: 37 (bottom); Walt Disney Co.: 32; **Carl V. Sissac/Sportslight:** 43 (top), 44 (right), 82 (top); **Sports Photo Masters/Sportschrome, Inc.:** 26.